THE LOCH

THE
LOCH

A year in the life of a Scottish loch

Roy Dennis

With specially commissioned photographs by Peter Moore

BBC Books

With very special thanks to the owners of the loch
for their generous permission to photograph and film
a year in the life of the loch.

This book is published to accompany the
television series entitled *The Loch*
which was first broadcast in Autumn 1993

Published by BBC Books,
a division of BBC Enterprises Limited,
Woodlands, 80 Wood Lane
London W12 0TT

First Published 1993
© Roy Dennis 1993

The moral right of the author
has been asserted

ISBN 0 563 36940 X

Designed by Tim Higgins

Set in Monotype Spectrum and Felix Titling
by Selwood Systems, Midsomer Norton
Printed and bound in Great Britain by BPCC Paulton Books Ltd, Paulton
Colour separation by Technik Ltd, Berkhamsted
Jacket printed by Belmont Press Ltd, Northampton

CONTENTS

INTRODUCTION

The freshwater lochs of Scotland are superb places, rich in history, wildlife and scenic beauty. It is believed that there are over 9000 freshwater lochs and lochans which are larger than three-quarters of an acre, and countless more that are smaller. This book is the story of one of those lochs, situated in the eastern half of the northern Highlands of Scotland. For our purposes, it is unnamed and its life is easily reflected in other lochs that I know well. In fact, their lives merge together as easily as a river running from one loch into another. I follow the life of the loch through the seasons, recognizing that beauty and interest are not solely located in rarity. It is the everyday changes that are of interest and fascination, if only we have time to understand and appreciate them. The choice of this loch was in a wildlife cameraman's mind. So used was he to dropping into exotic locations around the world to film for natural history programmes, that he wanted to show that it is not always necessary to travel to Antarctica or the Serengeti to experience the wonder of nature. On our doorstep are fascinating places that are only fully explored when we have seen them at dusk and at dawn, in high

OPPOSITE
*The peace and tranquillity of our loch is
enhanced by the grace and beauty of
a pair of mute swans.*

Introduction

summer and mid-winter, in howling gales and clammy fogs, in deep snow and on butterfly warm days, and a thousand other situations in between.

There is only one lake in Scotland: the Lake of Menteith north of Glasgow; the rest are lochs, with smaller ones being called lochans or dubh lochs. Around the coast, some marine inlets are called sea lochs; in fact, some of them are like small Norwegian fjords. This book, however, is about freshwater lochs. Scottish lochs vary tremendously in character, from the great, deep, foreboding waters, like Loch Ness and Loch Morar with their huge depths and stories of monsters, through open, fertile lochs set among rolling farmland, to the tiny hill lochans of remote peatlands and the high mountains. The variation is so great from west to east, from north to south, that our story is centred on the lochs of the eastern part of the Highland region, in particular those that are in the catchment of the Moray Firth and especially the lochs that are on the coastal plain or close to it.

Our loch is just an ordinary loch in many ways. The birds, mammals, fish, amphibians, insects and plants found there are to be seen on many lochs throughout the Highlands. Some of the wildlife found on other lochs is never seen here because the conditions are not right, while some creatures I see here will not be observed on other lochs in the district. This is a rich, busy loch, surrounded by lush vegetation and sheltered by fringing woodland of birches and pines. It has marshy islands covered with lichen-encrusted willow bushes and surrounded by sedges and bulrushes; this makes a great difference to wildlife.

There are similar lochs dotted throughout the lowlands surrounding the Moray Firth, often set in hollows left by the action of the ice-age glaciers and fringed by woodland and farms. They are usually productive lochs with a rich growth of reeds, sedges, bulrushes and flowering plants such as water lilies and bogbean. Often farm fields may run to the water's edge and human presence is frequent through fishing, walking and sometimes through water sports. The wildlife is often centred around wildfowl and waders, but nowadays these lochs are also frequented by hunting ospreys as well as ranging otters.

Introduction

There are two large lochs in this district. Loch Ness is a dramatic loch set between the mountains of the Great Glen. It is steep sided and was formed by the movement of the earth's tectonic plates. It is 24 miles long and plunges to nearly 900 feet in depth. This loch never freezes because of its depth; in fact, the inherent heat of the loch also provides a microclimate around the lochside and often the roads close to the loch remain ice free when most other roads are icy. Because of its steep sides it is rather poor for wildlife, with the exception of its alleged most famous inhabitant. The other large loch is much, much smaller and is very shallow compared to Loch Ness. It is only $1\frac{1}{2}$ miles long and half a mile wide, but Loch Eye is a haven for wildlife, especially in winter, when thousands of ducks, geese and swans use its water for feeding and roosting.

In the lower hills and glens, often set among forests of pines and birch woodlands, are a range of medium to small lochs; some are the most beautiful, picturesque lochs in majestic surroundings. The lochs nearest to my home nestle in the ancient Caledonian pine forest. They were created during the ice age by lumps of ice that slowly melted *in situ* during the glacial drift; they are called kettle-hole lochs. These lochs are not as productive as the low-ground lochs on the richer soils, as they tend to be more acid and peaty coloured, often with water the colour of whisky. But they are favoured haunts of some rare species, such as black-throated divers, Slavonian grebes and goldeneye ducks. In winter, they are often choice roosts for wildfowl and gulls during the night, affording the birds security and safety from scavenging foxes.

Finally, there are the high-level lochs and lochans nestling in the wide, bare moorlands and in the high mountains looking down on the Moray plain. Some are peaty pools fringed with red and green sphagnum mosses, with water so black that you can hardly see your hand through the freezing water. These pools are the nesting sites for red-throated divers and washing places for the plaintive golden plover of the heathery moors. The high mountain lochs are often crystal clear on a granite bed, almost devoid of plantlife. They are not wildlife lochs, but they add considerably to the beauty of wild places.

There is one thing that holds all these lochs together and that is

*As well as a wildlife haunt,
the loch is also a place for
people — patiently fishing
on a summer's evening or
coming in the morning
to feed the ducks.*

their deep relationship with the influence of weather, the true essence
of nature; bare branches against a red sunset, falling snow on peaty
black water, bright green delicate leaves luminescent in the spring
sunshine, sedges growing tawny and yellow in the autumn and
aquamarine ice on frozen lochs. My story is centred on one loch but
revives scenes and feelings gleaned from many lochs throughout a
lifetime's hiking these wild places.

My normal route to the loch is from the east. I park my car under

a pine tree below a small sandy cliff overlooking an old gravel pit. I walk about 50 yards through some pine trees to the edge of the loch. This is the easiest access point for visitors, for as soon as your presence is detected, the ducks and the swans start swimming towards you in anticipation of a free feed. Today about 30 mallards have come to the bank and are quacking very loudly to tell me they are hungry, but I actually know otherwise, for there is uneaten bread in the water and they have obviously been well looked after this morning. Some days, so many people come with food that the wildfowl can eat no more. The pair of mute swans are preening their snow-white plumage as they gently float in the still water. Soon they will be nesting on the island, but today there's time to rest after lunch.

A woodland path encircles the loch. In some places it is close to the water's edge and in others it meanders into the woodland. From a wildlife point of view, I'm not keen on paths which go right round lochs, for this gives no hiding places for sensitive birds and mammals to live and breed. Fortunately, our loch has secure bushy islands as a sanctuary. In several places alders and willows grow densely beside the water, so in the summer the loch is screened from the path. There's a choice of either walking to the right along the north side of the loch by way of a young pine wood or to the left along a wooded bank overlooking the loch. It's funny, but I nearly always go left and walk round the loch in a clockwise direction, or rather in the same direction as the sun. I wonder if that tendency is inherent in my genes from far-distant ancestors, to whom such things mattered. Two years ago, I was trekking in a remote region of Mongolia and I was struck that our guides walked diligently in a clockwise direction round the various religious sites that we passed on horseback. I was told it was unlucky to travel against the sun.

Today, I leave the ducks behind and walk up the woodland path to a high bank where I have one of the best views of the loch. From here I can see the whole loch. It is nearly a quarter of a mile in length from east to west, and about 200 yards wide. In size it is about 14 acres and its water is from rainfall and ground water, with no burns running into or out of the loch, just seepage through a marshy section at the north side and a wet hollow where water runs out through a wooded area on the south. From this high point, I can look away to the north towards the forested hills of Easter Ross; there are a few small crofts in the mid-distance, with blue smoke rising from one of the chimneys, suggesting a peat fire. It's nice to see this mix of woods, fields, moorland and water, with small farms nestling in the hollows among the forest. The ice age had a great effect on this low-lying area of gravel and sand, leaving a legacy of gravel ridges and wet hollows more than 10 000 years ago. The first hunters arrived

Introduction

about 3000 years later and this land has been inhabited by small farmers for well over 5000 years.

Directly in front of me are low islands, which in times of high water split into several separate islands; but normally there are only two marshy islands. They are well grown with bushy willow trees absolutely hanging with furry curtains of grey-green lichens. In winter the lichens are a real feature, especially when there's snow on the ground and the loch is frozen; in summer the velvety-green leaves take over and give a dense shape to the bushes. Sedges grow in profusion in the shallow water, with reeds, bulrushes and a spectacular array of water plants.

The south shore of the loch is edged with large willows, rowans, alders, birches and Scots pines; away to the south, through the trees at the top of the bank, is an open view to the coastal headlands of the Cromarty Firth and far, far in the distance I can see lingering patches of snow on the Cairngorm Mountains. At the west end of the loch stands a large Scots pine, well over 100 years old, which to me looks like a suitable osprey-nest tree; but I know that ospreys will never nest there, for it is far too close to the path where people walk. The north side of the loch is mainly birches of about twenty years old and a scatter of young Scots pine grows through them. On the north-east side is a bank of younger Scots pines growing thickly on a bracken bank with a few alders along the waterside.

The water today is very high; it is raining quite heavily now and there is the hissing noise of rain hitting the surface. As I look down from the bank I see that the water is very dark indeed. It is stained with peat as it seeps through the bog and, as a result, the loch is quite acid in character. Today the water surface is absolutely still, just a few chasing shadows caused by the wind touching the surface, and

---

OVERLEAF
A woodland path encircles the loch;
in some places it is close to the water's
edge, in others it meanders
into the woodland.

everywhere the plip plop of raindrops creates tiny little circles on the ebony surface of the water.

As I walk on round the loch, the coots are calling and one pair has decided to nest on a fallen branch beneath a willow bush on the island. It's too early yet to build, especially on a day of such high water, but in a couple of weeks' time they will be busy. The bramble bushes snag my progress on the south path and I admire the bright green stems of the blaeberries as I pass. The halfway point is at the far end of the loch. Looking back to the east, the land is flat and the horizon is marked by the trees near the car park; it is a vista of wide horizons and big skies. I often stop to look at the small forest bog on the homeward stretch. The ground here is swampy with sphagnum moss, cotton grasses and heather covering the ground where in summer various marsh plants flower. Scattered through the bogs are stunted Scots pine, nearly like bonsai trees because their feet are for ever soaked in peaty water and their growth is retarded. The whole walk is not much more than half a mile, yet the views and experiences change frequently on the path and there are many places to sit and watch and absorb this 'small town' loch.

I have a deep love of lochs. They seem to me to be the centre of activity in the land in which they are set. Life revolves around the water and so often the season's moods and each day's pace of life is best experienced close to the waterside. The loch closest to my home is very similar in size and shape to the loch described in this book. It is a loch of different moods as well. A walk to the loch in the evening light has always been a therapy for me after a stressful day at meetings or other worktime routines. The approach is part of the magic: knowing the exact spot, the exact tree or hillock from which you first see the silvery water shining in the distance. My usual route to my local loch follows no path; no sign of man is visible as I pass through Scots pines and birch scrub, knee-high heather and bog myrtle, fluffy with cotton grass in the spring. At one particular place, I can scan the mountains from the south-east through to the west, the native Caledonian forest all around me. There is not a single man-made structure in my view, no house, no road, no power line. I feel I am in a primeval forest bog in the Swedish wilderness and I

Introduction

imagine when this place too once echoed to the howl of wolves on crystal-clear nights of yesteryear. A high-flying jetliner may leave a white vapour trail in the sky but usually my view is pristine.

In the depths of winter, the countryside may be heavily cloaked in snow; silence is all-pervading. Tracks in the snow reveal where the animals have been travelling and what they have been doing. At times it is so cold that my nose is frozen, the air so frosty it is sore on my lungs. Here the lochs of the eastern Highlands emulate the lakes of Scandinavia and Russia in a deep icy grip. When the wind whips up, the snowdrifts pile against the far bank of the lochs, the ice is blown clear and the driven snow reaches every cranny of the countryside. Then suddenly, with hardly a warning, the wind changes to the west and a warm ocean breeze fans Scotland. This is the fresh thawing wind of Scotland and in no time the land and the lochs are freed of their frozen mantle of ice and snow.

Spring sees lengthening days, the ice has cleared from the water and the lochs regain their vitality after their winter sleep. Sometimes the blustery west wind fills the blue sky with billowing white clouds and there is a real feeling of change, or on still days the early-morning frost lifts from the ground in light wreaths of mist to reveal the most stunning of blue skies, crystal clear and everlasting. Summer days may be hot, heavy with the pollen of the Scots pine, dusty clouds blowing through the great woods and creating yellow whirls on the loch which are sometimes mistaken for oil pollution. The nights are short, often warm and balmy, the stars shaded by the sun shining from just below the northern horizon. Bands of clouds over the hills create beautiful sunsets and sunrises, which may be just a short flicker of colour or may last and last with ever-changing intensities of orange and red.

Late summer is often a time of rain; the heavy downpours of August soak the land, linked, some people say, to the advent of summer shows and Highland Games. Everywhere is sodden, the purple heather moors are misted over with low, clinging clouds and the ubiquitous midge is adding insult to injury. Soon the winged pests will be gone as the raging gales of late September sweep in from the Atlantic, testing the strongest of trees and the workmanship of builders. The first snows pepper the tops of the high mountains and, despite the Indian summer of October and the glorious colours of the deciduous trees, we are soon into the season of frosts and lengthening nights.

The value of a loch to wildlife is often influenced by its water chemistry as well as its location and physical character. In Scotland lochs may be nutrient rich (eutrophic) or nutrient poor (oligotrophic). In general the lochs lying in peaty areas on infertile rocks such as granite and gneiss are biologically rather impoverished, whereas freshwater lochs in the richer farming areas of red sandstones and limestone are nutrient rich. Some lochs, including our own, do not quite fit either of these two categories, for they are shallow and are rich in undecomposed plant material such as peat and humus. Their waters are acid and very peat stained.

Cold, deep lochs often have little plantlife, except maybe for some water lobelia growing in the shallow sand and gravel at the water's edge, but sheltered richer lochs have a wide range of plants growing in different micro-habitats in the loch. Green algae may be common in many lochs; created by sunlight, it is an important part of the whole water ecosystem. Truly floating plants, such as pondweed, occur in deeper water and merge into the plants, like water lilies, which have their roots in the bed of the loch. Then close to land come the emergent water plants, such as bulrushes and reeds, and as drier land is reached a whole array of marshland species grows in profusion: sedges, bogbean, yellow iris and water avens. These are joined by willows and alders, all of which are creating humus through leaf fall, leading ultimately to the raising of the ground level and eventually the drying out of the marsh.

The plants of the loch provide food and shelter for a rich variety of invertebrate creatures, which have their larval stage of life in the water and the adult stage as winged insects. The most spectacular are the dragonflies and damselflies, which enchant us in the summer as they speed about over the water in their dazzling array of colours, patterns and shapes. On the other hand, the most annoying are the clouds of midges and mosquitoes that rise from the same waters; at times on a damp summer evening they can be a real scourge. The

A roe deer on the heathery slope
above the loch in late summer.

---

loud hum of insects around our loch in summer reveals how rich freshwater lochs can be in the eastern Highlands; these insects provide important food for larger creatures.

There are brown trout which feed on aquatic insects in the water, rising on calm evenings to snap flying insects on the surface. In many Highland lochs, they leave the loch at spawning time to lay their eggs in the feeder streams, and there they may meet the migratory salmon. But our loch is never home to salmon or sea trout, although they pass less than a mile away as they travel up one of the fast rivers which lead from the firth to the mountain burns. Rainbow trout, from north America, have been introduced into some lochs. Pike are widespread in these low-ground lochs, probably introduced as a food fish many centuries ago. Perch have been released in a few lochs but are scarce this far north. Minnows, sticklebacks and eels are also present, but even so the variety of fish, available to predators such as ospreys, is the most impoverished in Europe.

Birds are the most obvious residents of our lochs; nearly 100 species may be seen or heard on or around any reasonably productive loch in the eastern Highlands in a year. Mallards are widespread and common, but most lochs will provide nesting, feeding or roosting sites for water birds such as grey heron, dabchick, mute swan, wigeon, tufted duck, goldeneye, teal, coot and moorhen. In winter they are joined by immigrants from northern lands, such as whooper swans, greylag and pink-footed geese. A few special lochs hold rare breeders such as the brilliantly coloured Slavonian grebe or the beautifully vocal black- and red-throated divers. Raptors are regular around the lochs, where they hunt for prey; the most spectacular is the osprey or fish hawk, which is now a regular hunter on many Highland lochs, including our own. Lots of small birds visit the loch. They may be residents such as the wrens and long-tailed tits which hunt for insects in the bulrush beds, or migrants such as swallows and swifts which on summer evenings swoop after flies above the water. No matter what time of the year I visit the loch, there's always a chance of being surprised by an unexpected avian visitor.

Finally there are the mammals, which as always are elusive and difficult to detect. Their presence is easier to see when snow-cover reveals their night-time journeys, but occasionally good views can be obtained if I am quiet and very observant, especially at times away from the heat of the day. Roe deer, rabbits, brown hares and red squirrels are most easily seen; foxes are smelt or heard more often than observed. On fine evenings, bats swoop over the loch or through the tree tops; they are difficult to identify, but pipistrelle, long-eared and Daubenton's bats all occur in the locality of the loch, and Natterer's bat is also recorded from this region. Moles, hedgehogs,

Introduction

voles, mice and shrews are common in the area but rarely seen well. Weasels and stoats live near the loch; I have seen a couple in the last year, including a stoat in its beautiful white ermine coat.

Pine martens have just recolonized the woods, while the low ground of Easter Ross is a favoured habitat for wildcats. These are majestic big tabby cats with boldly black-ringed tails. They are occasionally seen in summer when hunting rabbits for their young or in winter as they dash across the road in the headlights of my car. Sadly, many of our wildcats are now inbred with domestic cats, so some wildcats which look pure have a white patch indicating a doubtful parentage. Otters come to our loch on occasions, but it is too small and public to be used for breeding. These animals range from the coast to the larger rivers and lochs in the hills. This area is good for badgers, which build their extensive setts along the sandy ridges that run through the woodland. From there they can hunt for earthworms on the farmlands and bulbs and fruit in the woods.

On hot sunny afternoons in high summer, the life of Highland lochs belongs to us: children play in the white sands, the picnic is laid out on a large, warm grey rock, there's a happy domestic feeling. But as the sun sinks down over the mountains, we become less important and wild nature takes over once more. The loch is even more keenly a place of the wild when the northern lights flicker across the star-spangled sky of a freezing winter's night, when the surface of the loch is gripped in ice. Much more of the life of the loch takes place unseen by us than can be observed during our occasional visits. Nevertheless, what we do see makes these places special to us. The lochs are part of both us and the land, they delight us with their moods and their beauty, and the following chapters are celebrations of the four seasons of the year of a Highland loch.

SPRING

Clear bell-like notes cascade through the thin evening air and arouse a countryside still tired-looking after winter — the song thrushes are back! Spring is here. Country people use different signs to tell that spring has arrived: the first lambs, cattle being put out on grass, the first primroses flowering on a favourite bank or the first cuckoo calling from the hill. For me, song thrushes singing give a powerful feeling of the arrival of the new season and this evening, 7 March, they are singing their hearts out. Our song thrushes have spent the winter further south, especially in warmer south-west

The singing of a song thrush gives a powerful feeling of the arrival of a new season — soon the loch (opposite) is dappled by green leaves as the spring sun encourages new growth.

SPRING

Scotland, with some even living in the suburbs of Glasgow. They are one of the first birds to return from their winter quarters, the first usually arriving in late February and the rest in March. Often they all seem to come back *en masse*, because suddenly one evening there is a burst of sweet music drifting across the sour late-winter landscape. They are the heralds of spring, no going back, no false starts; winter is past.

This evening, as I walk round the loch, I hear my first song thrush of the year start to sing. I stop to listen to the beautiful melody, and further away in the bare birches I can hear another. It's such a calm evening that I can hear several others further on. I listen intently to the beautiful song, enjoying the sweet cadences of the song thrush's repertoire. I like song thrushes. They are not gaudily coloured, rather subdued and comfortable-looking birds with boldly spotted breasts and rich brown plumage. Their song, though, is most flamboyant. Song thrushes sing in repeated phrases of three or four crystal-clear notes, changing tune as they go along. Incidentally, some birds sing different phrases to others and in some parts of the country they have quite different dialects. It is easy to suggest words to fit the varied phrases in their delightful songs.

As this evening is so pleasant, I choose a seat below a big pine and look westwards to the setting sun across the loch in order to appreciate fully the beauty of this one songster. My mind is jogged, as it is every spring when I hear this song, to something which strikes me about the power of the notes: the question of land-ownership. This male song thrush definitely knows that he owns this particular section of woodland, skirting the northern part of the loch as far as the croft fields. As I listen carefully, his beautiful song says 'This-is-mine, this-is-mine, this-is-mine,' and then 'Go-away, go-away, go-away, go-away,' as well as other meaningful phrases in song-thrush language. Maybe to most people the song has no message except wild beauty, but it always means something to me. I know this bit of land belongs to some particular named person and I am sure that in the register of Sasines in Edinburgh there will be a legal document stating the ownership. To this song thrush, none of that makes sense; he does not believe in legal niceties, he believes in standing on the top of a tree and saying what he believes. And what he believes is that this is my territory and this is where I am going to sing my song and rear my family this year!

There is a truly beautiful sunset this evening, the sun sinking in a tremendous deep-red glow. It is absolutely still, it is warm, a quiet vibrancy of nature stirs in the air. The first flies of the year are out. I am not sure what they are called. They are very black and they do not come near me. They just jump up and down in the air, like yo-yos. They are also performing some kind of display, which obviously means something to other flies. More noticeably, the mallards are very busy on the loch, quacking and chattering with lots of duck small-talk, jostling and chivying each other. As dusk comes in, they start to leave the water. There is a deep, resonant quacking between the birds of each pair as they head off in twos and fours for secret pools and ponds in the twilight countryside. The drake mallards have had a busy day chasing off rival drakes from their ducks. This is the time when they are at their most attentive; even in the air they jostle for places and continue their noisy quacking.

Teal are calling from the marshy edge of the loch, a lovely little 'creeking' call. They will slip away later in the spring to nest in some secluded boggy marsh in the forest. Just before dusk, a pair of very handsome wigeon lands on the loch with a splash and for the briefest of moments they are framed by spreading circles of black ripples. The male is absolutely brilliant, his chestnut head topped by the brightest creamy-yellow crown, his darker reddish-brown breast and grey, black and white streaked body marked by a black patch at the stern. He displays a few times to his mate and then they take off for some place, maybe near, maybe far.

OVERLEAF
The deep red glow of a truly beautiful
sunset leaves the evening still and warm;
there is a quiet vibrancy of nature
stirring in the air.

SPRING

Now it is dark and the stars are bright and sparkling like winking diamonds in the sky. There is the tiniest glimmer of the moon, which will soon be rising, but it is only a half moon and not yet very bright. The owls are very vocal and, as I leave, one calls close by the lochside. There is a great deal of calling in the woods these nights as they voice their claims to their territories in a very expressive manner. All through the woodland the calls resound: one owl hoots and then another hoots further away, as though echoing on the hillsides above. Every now and then there is the harsher 'kewicking' call of a female having her say. The nearest pair has probably already decided where to nest – possibly in an old buzzard's nest, or maybe in a hollow tree or a convenient nest box put up by a thoughtful landowner or by a bird watcher.

At times there is total silence, probably because one of them has seen a movement of the forest floor. The male is always on the look-out for a nice juicy bank vole or wood-mouse to present to his mate. This is a sort of gift to cement the pair bond, but it is also important because at this season the female is in need of plentiful food so that she can build up her reserves to lay a clutch of white eggs. If rodents are plentiful, she might lay four or even five eggs, but if food is scarce she will lay fewer; if food is very scarce and it is just not a good year for voles and mice, she will not even bother to lay eggs. This year, I think it is quite good, as I have seen a number of mice and voles scampering across the road in the lights of my car. A little earlier this evening on my walk there was a rustle in the leaves as the most beautiful little reddish-brown bank vole dashed across the path and into its burrow.

The wading birds have also come back. They are very obvious arrivals in spring. I saw my first lapwings a week or so ago as they came tumbling out of the western sky with their big, flappy, butterfly wings flashing black and white as they slanted against the grey shoulder of a hill. They are still in flocks; in fact, there were nearly 120 of them in the first flock that I saw. It will be a few days before the pairs start to break up and reclaim the little marshy fields and bogs where they nest. Then, one clear cool night, the first oyster-catchers arrived. It is interesting how often they seem to return at night. There is a sudden piercing whistle, a whistle that I have not heard inland for nearly six months since they left last summer. 'Squeak, squeak' they cry as they inspect the various breeding fields that were used last year.

Here in the Highlands, although oystercatchers are common nesting birds around the coast, good numbers also nest inland, scattered across the farm fields as well as beside open lochs and along gravel banks in the big rivers. This loch is not suitable for oyster-catchers: it is muddy and is surrounded by vegetation; it is tucked away in the woodland, so the only time oystercatchers appear is when they fly from the farm fields to wash in the gravel pit. Later in the summer, when the mud is exposed on the island, a little family party may drop down just for a few hours. Our oystercatchers spend their winters in western England, their favourite places being the Ribble and Mersey estuaries and Liverpool Bay. I often think of the contrast between leaving Liverpool one day and arriving in the Highlands the next.

Tonight I heard a pair of curlews calling and also my first woodcock rhoding or displaying. This plump brown crepuscular wader nests in the local birch woods. They fly like ghostly shapes at dusk, crossing the loch on their territorial patrols, giving a little snort and a grunt as they go along the sylvan pathways that have been travelled by woodcocks in previous springs.

The moss crop feast

There is a change in the weather – it is suddenly, perceptibly milder. Tonight there is a soft fresh wind blowing from the south-west. I recognize this fresh wind of the Highlands: it is a noisy wind, an awakening wind which stirs the trees and melts every last remaining drop of ice on hidden hollows in the woods. It is a true sign of spring, and everything feels the urge to shake off its winter coat and don the pale, delicate mantle of spring. Among the first signs of spring growth are the spiky heads of the moss crop or cotton grass. This very showy sedge grows in wet places throughout the Scottish Highlands. It is easily recognized later in the summer,

SPRING

*Small rodents are plentiful around
the loch — a bank vole drinks at
the water's edge.*

*In early spring, the moss crop
is eagerly sought out by hungry birds
and mammals — later in the summer
the fluffy snow-white heads of
the cotton grass wave in the wind.*

when wet moorlands are a sea of snowy-white heads blowing in the wind. But in early March they are only starting to push through the wet marshes; the first evidence of actual growth is when the tiny, dark, blackish-grey head starts to poke up through the old vegetation.

Many different animals and birds wait for the moss crop to appear, and then one day, as if a signal has been given, it is ready. Suddenly there is almost a stampede converging on the mosses: roe and red deer, blue and brown hares, sheep and cattle, capercaillies and black grouse, as well as just about every animal that eats vegetation, are seeking this delicacy. They have learnt from long, long ago that the way to eat moss crop is to be gentle. They hold the top of the flower head, gently pull upwards and out comes a 4- or 5-inch stem of succulent growth. The top is like a little feather duster, but the long stem is pale and yellowy-green. It is the first succulent bite after the survival rations of late winter, which is why it is so eagerly sought after. The cattle and sheep love it and at this time of the year they plod off to the bogs to feed. Some of the old people say that it is not particularly nutritious, but that it fills the animals' bellies at a time of year when they are often hungry, so it is a welcome change from eating hay, which has been their staple diet since last November. The deer like the moss crop very much. Roe deer, especially, are so beautiful to watch as they step daintily through the wet mosses, gently plucking the moss crop.

This morning I visited the local heronry, which is about 10 miles from the loch. The herons have nested in a plantation of 30-foot Scots pines for at least the last ten years. There is a convenient hill above the wood and from there it is possible to look down into the nests. You have to be very careful, because if you appear too suddenly the herons fly out with much calling and you know you've caused panic. Today I gently inched my way behind a large tree, from where, with my binoculars, I looked down on to the wood a quarter of a mile away. The herons were already nesting, with quite a lot of displaying taking place, their beautiful plumes being thrown forward as two herons faced each other, clattering their bills in a kind of sabre-rattling call which echoed across the top of the wood.

I saw that several nests already held incubating birds, while other herons were still nest-building. I carefully showed myself and the birds nervously stood up. I made a quick count of the number present before hurriedly withdrawing so they could settle again. There were six nests with three eggs, three with two eggs and four pairs still to lay. This is about average for this little heronry and they seemed well on the way to another successful season. Quite often at this time of the year herons eat frogs: this is the easiest season to catch them as they congregate in their favourite pool to breed.

The frogs are quite difficult to see in the loch, because it is mostly dark and deep, but in one of the shallower bays is a whole group leaping and splashing about. You have to be very quiet as you walk towards them because they are surprisingly alert and if they are alarmed then all you see are the ripples on the water as they dive to hide in the mud and vegetation below the surface. But if I walk very quietly and sit gently on the bank above this particular place, I soon see the frogs swimming in the cloudy water. Slowly they return and carry on with the business of display. Some are giving their mating calls, their throats blowing up to produce beautiful croaking calls which carry a long distance. I remember once hiking in the mountains when I heard frogs calling at an altitude of nearly 3000 feet. I tracked them to a small hill loch nearly a mile away. They were in full mating frenzy in the shallows while the other end of the loch was still imprisoned in ice.

Back in the warmer water of our loch the successful males are holding tightly on to their mates, the forelegs clasped across the female's back. Some females have already laid their eggs, with masses of frogspawn floating in the water. This is a particularly good place for the frogs to spawn because soon there will be plenty of algae in the water for the young tadpoles to eat. There are also plenty of places for them to hide and room in the whole loch for them to grow up until they become real frogs and leave the water in the summertime. I often think that frogs are either incredibly careless or very skilled at taking advantage of every opportunity, for on my walks through forests and fields I sometimes come across frogspawn in tiny pools of water which have formed in the tracks of a large vehicle that passed during the winter. It is wet and well flooded in March, but later in the spring I find it dried up and the frogspawn dead. There are advantages for the frogs in using shallow pools, because the water is warmed more quickly by the sun and the young frogs hatch earlier.

Toads also breed in the loch, but they tend to keep to themselves in a different part of the water. They also seem to be more careful, because I never see toadspawn lying around in temporary pools, although in general they prefer to lay their eggs in cooler water. Toadspawn is quite unlike frogspawn: it is laid in long chains hanging in the underwater vegetation rather than in great big masses.

Kites on the wing

It is late March now; in fact, we are past the spring solstice and the days are now longer than the nights. It seems to be a headlong rush into real spring. The days lengthen, especially in the evenings, and there is suddenly time to do all those things you wish you could have done outside in winter but were unable to do because of the lack of daylight. Now, often it is a struggle to come in as dusk approaches, because spring evenings in the Highlands are just so very, very special.

Today there are lovely, puffy white clouds in a blue sky, with a gentle breeze, the ideal weather for displaying buzzards. In this area there are many buzzards; they are often in the sky and this afternoon they are very obvious indeed. There are two over there, just above the western end of the loch, circling together on broadspread wings, about 200 feet above the trees. They give mewing calls and are engrossed in each other as the courtship flight intensifies. Their underparts are white patterned with dark brown and their wings are outstretched. Slowly, the smaller male bird gains height; he is now twice as high as the female in the sky. Suddenly he closes his wings and dives steeply down towards the female. Well before he reaches her, he opens his wings and soars upwards, then down again in a dive and up again, throwing himself through the sky in his wild roller-coaster display. I presume she is impressed, but I do know that other buzzards nearby will see him in display and take note that this home range is occupied.

SPRING

Only a few weeks ago the buzzards were still sitting around on fenceposts and feeding on worms in the wet winter fields on the farmland. Then spring was a long way away, and breeding activities were confined to the occasional visit to their old nest sites. Buzzards generally use the same nests year after year, each spring choosing one of their old nests and renovating it with new sticks and grasses; there they will lay three or four brown-blotched eggs in April. At present it is still too early for egg-laying and there is plenty of time for aerial exhibitions.

I wish I had been by the loch the other day, because one of my friends was passing this way and saw a red kite. He had been watching a pair of buzzards displaying above the loch when a third bird joined in the soaring; he was thrilled to see that it was a kite. It was the first he had seen in this particular area. He knew that it was one of the kites that we had released in a special reintroduction project carried out in the Highlands. The red kite used to be a common bird in Scotland, like elsewhere in the British Isles, but in the last century the Victorian gamekeepers and sportsmen decided that all birds of prey and predatory mammals should be removed from the face of the earth. So every means was set against these birds and animals — traps, poisons and guns were used and in no time at all their numbers started to fall.

The kites were particularly prone to destruction because they were so used to people and tended to be confiding, coming to places where people lived and worked. By the end of the nineteenth century, almost every kite in Scotland had been destroyed, except for one or two pairs which survived to nest until the early years of this century and then they too were gone. In fact, virtually all the red kites in Britain were exterminated during that period, along with other raptors such as the sea eagle, osprey and goshawk. Just a tiny reservoir of survivors remained to nest in central Wales. Although occasional kites were seen in Scotland on migration, probably birds which had accidentally crossed the North Sea from Germany or Sweden, none ever showed a sign of returning to breed, nor was there any likelihood of successful natural recolonization.

Five years ago the Royal Society for the Protection of Birds (RSPB)

The red kite, locally known as the salmon-tailed gled, has returned to the Highland skies, thanks to the successful re-introduction project.

and the Nature Conservancy Council (NCC) started a joint project to return the kite as a nesting bird in both Scotland and England. I was fortunate to be involved with the Scottish end of the project, and over the last four summers I have travelled each spring to Sweden, where the Swedish authorities and ornithologists have kindly allowed me to collect young kites to bring back for release in Scotland. So far, we have transported sixty-nine young kites from Sweden to Scotland and successfully reared them in captivity for about five weeks before allowing them to fly free in the wild. The young kites have survived exceptionally well; most of them have stayed nearby in winter, though some have travelled to southern Scotland and a few wanderers have ventured as far as Yorkshire and Cornwall, while three went as far as Ireland. Sadly, some died on their travels, but most have headed back to the Highlands as spring calls. They have survived much better than we expected and over 75 per cent have lived through to the following summer.

Last summer a pair of kites, only two years old, started to build a nest. We had not expected them to nest until they were at least three or four years of age. They built a most superb nest in a big conifer tree and in April laid three eggs. We kept clear of the nest at that stage, but we could see the female's head over the edge as she incubated through that month. One exceptionally exciting day we found her with young. The pair hatched three young, but sadly the period after hatching was very wet and they managed to rear only one chick. What an important chick it was — a real landmark in the project and the first young kite to be reared in Scotland for nearly 100 years! This summer we will return again to Sweden and bring back another twenty-four young to Scotland for release. We also expect more nests from the birds that have now matured. At the moment the situation is looking very encouraging and it is likely that we will have red kites once again as a regular breeding bird in Scotland.

Kites often spend time with buzzards, just like the one above the loch, because they rarely kill their own food. They prefer to scrounge scraps off someone else, either a gull, crow or a buzzard. Quite often a buzzard will take a dead rabbit, killed by a car, off the road and will eat most of the remains. When perhaps only one end of a leg is left, along comes a kite with its beautiful buoyant flight, snatches the remaining morsel and makes off to feed in a tree. There seems to be little meat left after the buzzard's meal but I suppose the leftover leg of a rabbit is not something to turn your nose up at if you're a kite. As scavengers they are well fed.

I expect one day in the future they may even nest again around here, where once, long ago, kites would have been seen. When the people on the hill crofts had cut their corn by hand, over 100 years ago, and the golden fields were covered in stooks, it is very likely that they would have admired the beautiful fluttering, gliding flight of red kites as they searched for voles amongst the fields of stooks. To them the bird was known as the salmon-tailed gled.

Creatures of the dark

Tonight I decided to walk by the water. As I set off along the dark pathways from the car park, there was a reasonable amount of light once my eyes had got used to the dark. More and more we are losing our ability to travel at night without artificial light; yet less than 100 years ago our ancestors were far more knowledgeable and at home with the night sky. I sometimes think, on star-spangled nights like this, that television screens are such poor substitutes for the great span of the night sky.

It is quiet and still and I can hear the frogs calling even though I am still quite some distance from the their haunts. I can hear the creaking call of a teal and some sharp quacking from the mallards, and even a little gabble of noise from the mute swans, wondering who is trespassing around the loch after dark: 'How the heck can silly

OVERLEAF
Gulls follow the tractor at dusk.
The spring-time ploughing provides
excellent food for the gulls just as they
prepare to nest and lay eggs.

people feed us if they come at the wrong time of the day!' Now I hear the screaming call of a water rail; it makes me stop and listen hard. It is a comparatively small bird to have such a fearsome call, a screaming wail coming from the reed bed as if someone were being strangled.

Further away I can hear an absolute clamour of gulls; I guess at this time of the year there may be 10 000 black-headed gulls roosting on the larger loch some miles away. Between leaving their winter haunts and nesting in the marshes, the gulls gather in huge, tightly packed communal roosts on large freshwater lochs in the late afternoons. As they arrive for the night, the dense flocks can look like pack-ice on the grey waters. In early spring I can hear a roost from my house and when I go out last thing at night to close in the hens from the foxes, I can hear the black-headed gulls calling, grumbling and bickering away all night long on the loch. They are one of the noisiest birds I know, seeming to keep up a constant racket all through the night.

In the early morning the gulls set off to scour the countryside for food and it's fortunate that spring ploughing is taking place on farms and crofts in the district. Nowadays there is less spring cultivation because many of the larger farms grow winter wheat and barley, which is planted in the autumn rather than the spring. The small fields on the hill crofts above the loch are now being ploughed and one day I looked up and saw nearly 100 gulls following an old blue tractor turning the soil ready for oats to be sown in a few weeks' time. The gulls were swooping down to take earthworms thrown up by the plough. It is very important for the female gull to obtain a rich food supply so that the eggs can be successfully formed in her body. Occasionally the plough may dislodge a mouse from its underground nest: that really is a prize for a fortunate gull. If the bird doesn't swallow the mouse quickly, an almighty scrum of tussling white birds try to steal the tasty morsel from each other.

Nowadays even the buzzards follow the plough hoping for mice, or even making do with juicy worms. A pair of oystercatchers was also walking on the freshly turned ground. In a few weeks they will lay their eggs in a small hollow in the ground, usually in the stoniest part of the field. By that time, the farmer will have smoothed out the field with harrows and the only task to finish after the corn has been sown will be to roll the field. From the tractor it is easy to find the oystercatcher's nest: each time you pass, the bird runs off its nest. Most people mark its exact position with a stone marker so that they can avoid breaking the eggs. Once the heavy rollers have done their job, the stones are removed and the oystercatcher can return to her three beautifully camouflaged eggs.

This is the time of year when moles seem to be particularly active, or possibly it's just that their activities are so obvious. One day the newly planted field is smooth and perfectly rolled; the next morning the delicate green lines of newly sprouted oats, glistening with dew drops, are marred by a straggling line of mole heaps, perfect mounds of black earth. No wonder farmers loose the rag and hasten to the shed for a mole trap, because moles throw up stones as they excavate and these can damage the blades of the combine harvester later in the summer. Occasionally I see a mole run by the lochside path, for they are quite at home in grassy swards under mature deciduous trees.

Fresh April days

It is April today and the loch is looking tranquil. The sedges are already a fragile green, shiny new stems poking up out of the water amongst the tawny folded stems and leaves of last year. There are clumps of tussock grass in the water in some places, still mainly yellow in the low morning light, but with a greenish tuft emerging from the crown. Signs of new life are everywhere. The bog myrtle plants appear very orangey-brown as their buds start to swell. A furtive pair of moorhens is busily scuttling around in the thin reeds

OVERLEAF
*By the middle of April willows
at the edge of the loch sprout
fresh spring foliage.*

at the far end, flicking their white-edged black tails as they search for food. The frogs are plopping and croaking and splashing in one little area of sedge. I can hear the coal tits seesawing in the wood behind me.

If I turn more towards the south, the water is mirrored in reflections around every single stem of sedge. The water, though, is still cold, with just a few flies rising above the surface. There is a pond skater moving around on the surface, but he's not particularly frisky, just moving in little circles of maybe 10 inches. I don't think he's finding a lot to eat this morning. It is warm in the direct sunlight, but every now and then there is just that little breeze which still has a thinness and a coldness to it. Further away a crow calls in the wood, cawing as always with much grating defiance. Every now and then the pair of crows come to check for scraps where people feed the swans. At this time of the year they are nearly as adept as the ducks at getting food, and if any bread is left over and washes to the edge of the water then the crow is very quickly down there. Already they are busy preparing their nest at the top of a tall, solitary Scots pine, ready for the eggs that will follow in a few weeks.

Staring down really closely into some rather deeper water amongst the sedges, I can see a newt swimming; this looks like a palmate newt, which is the commonest species in this area. We have all three species of newts living in the ponds and lochs of the eastern Highlands, but in most areas we are unsure of their distribution. It is quite difficult to know which species are in which lochs, unless you make a special effort. As a child I was a keen newt-catcher: with a tiny piece of meat attached to a thin thread I could gently pull to the bank a newt holding tightly to his meal. A pike glides through the stems of the sedges – a very distinctive arrow of ripples, as he moves through the water. Pike enjoy this type of loch and there is a good population of them in the Highlands. This species was introduced to Scotland many centuries ago when the fish were reared in ponds for food. Now a little party of siskins is flying over, chattering in the wind, and a curlew is bubbling enthusiastically from the farm fields above the lochs. The lambs are calling to their mothers from the fields; most of them are newborn, as the lambs are now coming thick and fast on the farms. It is just a joy to be out on this beautiful morning.

SPRING

A pair of starlings was nesting today, but they were not seriously concentrating on the job; they were sort of spring-cleaning a nest box. They had chosen a box far too big for themselves; it was one of the old owl nesting boxes, with a hole big enough to accommodate a tawny owl. The tawny owls nested in this box several years ago, but this year it is unoccupied. It does, however, have a bed of sawdust on the floor. We always put several inches of sawdust in the bottom of these large boxes to make them attractive to owls, but the starlings have taken robust exception to it and are flying out of the box with beaks full of sawdust and dropping it on the water. Once they clear it out – goodness knows how many days it is going to take them – they will start to build their own untidy nest of grasses, moss and feathers. It fits their scientific name: *Sturnus vulgaris*.

Starlings may be common birds in the city, but at nesting time they are quite well dispersed. In the countryside they prefer to nest in areas where there are farms, especially mixed farms where cattle still graze the fields. They are particularly attracted to the various insect larvae that live in cattle droppings and you see them marching around on the grass digging their bills into the cowpats. They know exactly when a cowpat is ready to investigate, maybe a week after it was dropped on the ground by a cow. By that time it has been colonized by the special insects which live in cattle dung. There will be beetles and flies and all will provide a veritable feast of grubs for the starlings. From here they fly backwards and forwards with cargoes of food for their young. But those days are still a long way in the future; now it is time to build their nest.

They have to be careful nesting in these boxes, because another creature has found that owl boxes make particularly attractive homes. The other squatter is the pine marten. This large member of the weasel family, which is so accomplished at climbing trees, finds large nest boxes the most luxurious of dens. Thirty years ago, I remember it was extremely difficult to see a pine marten in Scotland and I searched for them in their last strongholds in the rocky mountainsides of Wester Ross without success. In the last two decades, however, the fortunes of the pine marten have totally changed. No longer is it persecuted as it was in Victorian times. The large areas of new forests

*The pine marten is now widespread
in northern Scotland after being nearly
exterminated in the last century; they
sometimes take over lochside nesting boxes
erected for breeding ducks.*

planted by the Forestry Commission have favoured the animal and it has thrived and spread. In fact, its range has spread from west to east: you can even see pine martens on the outskirts of Inverness, running across the road and dashing into the top of an old shed, where they may have a den. They make their dens in a variety of places: in big jumbles of rocks on stony hillsides, in hollow trees, or in the nests of large birds. I know of several golden eagle eyries where the nest has grown so big that pine martens can burrow in the bottom of the eyrie and the eagles nest on the top. Surprisingly, they appear to be good neighbours.

Martens have also learnt to use nest boxes. One spring, a friend of mine found a brood of pine martens when he was checking his owl boxes. His discovery did not win him a particularly warm welcome. As he clung to the tree and put his hand in to check the contents there was a most almighty noise — a kind of spitting, chittering buzz of anger. He quickly dived down the tree, as the irate adult pine marten looked out. Obviously there were youngsters in the nest and he offered to show them to me. So we went along a few days later and looked into the box, but we were too late: the pine marten had realized that her den had been discovered. She had transported her young to another, safer site. One by one, she would have carried them by the neck through the forest, maybe up and down trees, repeating the journey until her family was safely denned again.

Pine martens eat just about anything and at this time of the year they are particularly fond of frogs, birds' eggs and young birds, or any living creature that they can catch. It might be a fish in a shallow bit of the river, or a nice bank vole that fails to reach the safety of its burrow, or even sometimes a red squirrel, which they corner in the tops of the trees. Later on in summer, pine martens change their diet to fruit, especially the navy-blue succulent fruits of the blaeberry, and in between times they scavenge in the litter bins of Highland picnic sites.

The birches are now turning green. The birch tree in spring has the most beautiful delicate green tinge as it comes into leaf. One day there is no leaf, and then next day the leaf tips have broken and the trees have this fragile green image. The leaves take several days to grow and I like the period when they are just tiny ears of leaves showing on the trees. I recall a lovely story told me by a friend whom I had met by the river bank. He is a keen fisherman and was quite far up the river when we stopped to chat. He noticed that the leaves of the birch were just breaking, which he said was a really good sign, because the salmon never get to this section of river until the birch leaf is the size of a mouse's lug and that was just the size they were that day. He never caught a fish while I was with him to prove the point, but we both enjoyed looking at the soft green lugs of the birch trees.

The mallard in the bramble bush

The loch is a sea of green today, the waterside bushes and trees, with their sprouting fresh green leaves, overhanging the glassy surface. Primroses! The very first primroses — a delight of yellow and green nestling in a sunny hollow. I kneel down on the wet mossy ground just to smell pure sweet primroses — I inhale deeply of the fragrance of spring. Nearby a clump of verdant celandines are close to opening their bright yellow flowers; it has been a struggle for them, but they are almost blooming. To add to the magic, a willow warbler is singing. This one is the first I have heard this year and for the next few days I expect I will hear one or two in various places that I visit. Then suddenly one night they will arrive *en masse* from Africa and the following morning the song of willow warblers will echo through the woodlands in the Highlands. This bird has such a lovely little song when he first arrives in the spring: a sweet little trilling cadence of notes. The trees around the loch are just right for them; they do not like mature woodland or dense plantations, but where there are scattered trees, marshy places, open ground with paths and long grass on the ground, the willow warblers find suitable nesting places. They build a lovely little wren-like nest on the ground, amongst the long vegetation, where they lay seven or eight tiny speckled eggs.

Today's bird is finding a few insects attracted to the flowers of a big spreading willow, which is a riot of powdery pollen catkins. In only a month's time he will be hurriedly collecting caterpillars from the trees around the loch and popping down every few minutes to feed his ravenous young. Then the warblers have a quite different call. Walking around the loch you come too close to a nest and the birds perch in a tree above you, flicking their wings nervously and anxiously calling 'wheet, wheet', wishing you would go on your way.

This morning I had a lucky break. As I walked along one of the paths at the far end of the loch, near a rather wet area, suddenly I spotted a dark shining eye through the tangle of an old bramble bush. Immediately I saw the feathered outline of a female mallard sitting on her nest. She was so perfectly still, so expertly camouflaged and so evidently comfortable on her bed of dead leaves and grasses that I had no wish to give away the fact that I had seen her. So I did not stare at her too intently, as she might easily leave her nest in panic and the eggs be predated. I just noted the nest's position in my memory and walked on. I would look again on my return.

This evening she is off her nest, presumably away feeding on the loch. You could not tell that there was a nest there at all. Before leaving, she had carefully pulled the dead leaves and the grasses over her nest, but I could see just the tiniest hint of the buffy-brown down from her body which she has used to line the nest to keep the eggs warm. Just this one time I will have a quick look. I carefully pull back the lining over the top of the nest and see that she is sitting on twelve greenish-blue eggs. They are large eggs really, and they feel lovely and warm. I will follow their progress over the next few weeks.

Nest-building

There is time to sit on a high bank overlooking the loch: it is just the most beautiful scene. It is a superb spring morning, with not a single cloud in the baby-blue sky and the warmth of the day already to be felt. The drake mallards are in a huddle on the edge of the island, some washing, some just roosting on the mud. One female briefly came down for a drink and was chased by a whole gang of amorous drakes. She soon retreated into the woodland to her nest, where peace and quiet reigns. I wonder if she is my bramble-bush duck, as I call her.

OPPOSITE
The willow warblers have returned from Africa en masse *and
their songs echo from the willows and birches. The pollen bright
catkins (above) and fresh green leaves of willows by
the lochside provide feeding and cover for the warblers.*

The coots are busy nest-building, the sedges have now started to
grow quite lustily and there is a lovely green flush all across the edge
of the loch and the islands, instead of the drab winter browns and
greys. There is a real feeling of growth and promise. One pair of coots
has nested in an overhanging willow bush and another in amongst
the newly sprouting bulrushes. They go backwards and forwards,
diving down and pulling up vegetation from the bottom of the water
and dragging great strands of bogbean roots and old lily leaves to
make their big bulky nests. Once they swam past a pair of dabchicks,

or little grebes, who are undertaking their spring activities in a much more subdued way. At this time of the year the dabchicks look their very best as well. They are small birds, really, quite dumpy, but beautifully marked in the spring. Their heads are nearly black and they have the most gorgeous rich chestnut sides to their faces and the fronts of their necks, as well as the most brilliantly coloured yellow gape to the base of their bills. They have very special displays, with whinnying calls and little dashes across the surface, leading sometimes to excited underwater chases. This is an ideal loch for dabchicks and at least one pair always have their nest here.

Dabchicks are not as brilliantly coloured as the Slavonian grebes, which breed on some of the lochs in the Highlands, but not this one. This is a much rarer bird as well, with only about sixty to seventy pairs nesting in the whole of Great Britain. Slavonian grebes first started to nest in the Scottish Highlands in the early part of this century and prefer rather larger lochs with thick beds of sedges, particularly the bottle sedge, where they make their floating nests. They are most spectacularly coloured, with incredible orange tufts on the sides of their heads, which they can erect in display. The neck and sides of the body are a rich chestnut red. They perform the most incredible displays; the pair face each other and fan the tufts on their faces and shake their heads towards each other while rising out of the water in the most beautiful of dances, continuously serenading each other with whinnying calls.

There was the ripple of a brown trout rising to the surface of the water just now. The warmer water touched by the sun's rays has persuaded the trout to leave their dark, deeper winter haunts. The increasing amount of pond life is also to their liking: water boatmen, caddis-fly larvae and a whole range of aquatic invertebrates are starting to appear in the water. A common sandpiper, a long-distance migrant from Africa, called briefly on the muddy bank of the island just now; it gave a few calls, a few whistles, ran along the mud, bobbing its tail, its dark brown and white plumage flashing, and then soared off on its journey, probably to one of the rivers in the mountains nearby. There is also a cuckoo calling. I heard my first a few days ago at home, but this is the first one that I have heard near the loch.

SPRING

Scandinavian cousins

May Day today, with dewy dawn to splash on my face. The pair of mute swans are well into their incubation period. The female is sitting tightly on her great big nest on the island and the cob has been guarding her for nearly ten days as she sits on her eggs. It will still be about three weeks before the eggs hatch. I do not know how many eggs they have, but it will be four, five or six, and they really are big greeny-white ones. They will be guarded extremely well: the male is a very determined defender of his territory and he will not let anything near his nest, not even innocent mallards or coots, which are of no danger at all. Nothing must disturb or distress his mate. She is a tough character as well and will easily be able to defend her eggs from a straying fox.

Here in the earthy bank, just 3 feet above the water's edge, under the roots of an old gnarled alder tree, a robin flew out as I passed. I looked carefully in the bank and there was a beautifully constructed nest containing five pinky-brown eggs nestling in a hole where a large stone had been dislodged in the winter.

An unobtrusive little duck landed on the water as I straightened up from the robin's nest and started to dive in the shallows further along. It was a brownish-grey little bird with a white flash in its wing and I easily recognized it as a female goldeneye. This is a diving duck, which does usually visit this particular loch briefly but is nowadays quite common on some other lochs in the Highlands.

Goldeneyes have always been common visitors to Scotland and thousands of them winter in various places around the coast, as well as in good numbers inland on the big lochs and rivers. In springtime, all of these birds used to travel north to nest in Sweden, Norway and Finland, but nowadays we have some nesting with us in the Highlands. It's a fascinating story. I remember may years ago, in fact in 1961, I saw a female goldeneye on a loch near my home in Strathspey. She had with her one duckling, but I knew that the goldeneye had never nested in our country. When I looked carefully at the duckling, I realized that it was not the goldeneye's young but that she was being 'aunty' to a stray tufted duckling which had attached itself to her.

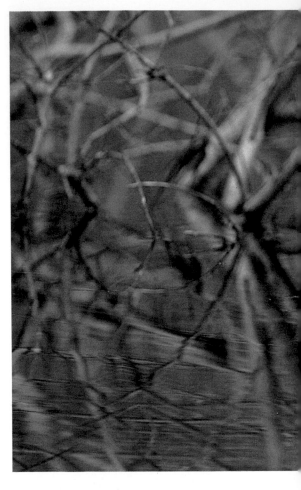

BELOW
*A female mallard incubates twelve eggs
in her warm downy nest; her dark shining
eye attracted my attention.*

OPPOSITE BELOW
*Displaying goldeneye drakes are
spectacular and nowadays can be seen
on many Highland lochs in springtime.*

RIGHT
*Another rare breeding species is the
Slavonian grebe, which also has a
beautiful plumage and attractive
breeding displays.*

Nevertheless, this encouraged us in the RSPB to try to persuade this very attractive bird to nest in Scotland. Every spring, the winter visitors from Scandinavia had been staying on later and later into early May, and in a few favourite places we would see them displaying in their most dramatic way.

The male, unlike the female, is the most brightly patterned bird imaginable, principally black and white but with a very distinctive green-tinged head, a brilliant golden eye – hence its name – and, between the eye and the bill, a very obvious white oval patch. The legs are red and the bill is black. The female has a brown head and a yellow eye, and when she is in breeding plumage she has a little pinkish-yellow tip to her bill. The male birds have very elaborate courtship displays in the spring and a distinctive creaking call.

We knew that in Scandinavia goldeneyes traditionally nest in holes in trees, but that for more than two centuries they had also nested in big nest boxes tied to trees in Swedish forests. These boxes were originally put up along rivers long ago by woodsmen, who wanted to have a supply of fresh eggs for breakfast when they floated timber down the rivers. Some nesting boxes for goosanders and goldeneyes had been erected beside Highland lochs in the late 1950s, but without success. After my sighting of the female goldeneye with the tufted duckling in 1961, we in the RSPB started a new nest-box project for goldeneyes around suitable lochs in the Highlands. Over the years, our boxes were used by tawny owls and jackdaws, redstarts and pied wagtails, red squirrels and starlings, and in later years by pine martens, but never a sign of a goldeneye duck. That was until July 1970, when a visiting birdwatcher to Strathspey came across a female goldeneye with four black and white young on a small loch. The following year, the same female nested again in the same place but lost her young, probably killed as they made their journey from the nesting area towards the river. Then in 1972 nine young ones successfully reached the water; in 1973 there were three nests; by 1976 eight nests; by 1979 twenty-one nests; and by 1984 the population had increased to over fifty pairs. Now there are more than 100 nesting goldeneyes in the Highlands each year and they are increasing rapidly. It is satisfying also to learn that they are dispersing to colonize new areas.

SPRING

In natural circumstances, as I have said, goldeneyes nest in hollow trees or in holes made in trees by the large black woodpecker of Europe. But here in Scotland we have relatively few holes in trees, because so many of the older trees are cut down before they have time to provide nesting holes for birds, or roosting sites for bats. The nest boxes are placed in trees to simulate natural holes and the ducks find them very attractive indeed. The inside of the nest box has a layer of 2–3 inches of sawdust, in which the birds can lay their eggs. The females come to the boxes in mid-April to start laying. Each female will lay eight to twelve eggs. They are large greeny-blue eggs and the female lines the box with beautiful soft down once she has completed her clutch. Goldeneyes have a very unusual nesting behaviour. Younger females, instead of always having their own nest, will sometimes come and dump eggs in another duck's box. We think these 'dumpers' are probably young birds, related to the female who is nesting in the box. Quite often when we have been doing our monitoring studies, we have checked the boxes and found up to fifteen or twenty eggs in a box, with the maximum so far being twenty-eight eggs. Such a large clutch had probably been laid by three or even four females.

Nevertheless, females incubate these large clutches just as if they were their own, and the maximum number of young we have known to fledge from one box is eighteen. Normally, about nine or ten youngsters are encouraged to jump out of the box the day after they hatch when they are all dry and bright-eyed. They are tiny little balls of black and white fluff, very beautiful and independent little ducklings. The female then takes them to the water; in the case of boxes overhanging the water, the journey is very short indeed – just vertical! But sometimes the nest boxes may be up to a mile from water and then the mother gathers together her little band and walks them towards the water. Quite often they will use a small loch for the first few days of their life, where the young ones dash around amongst the edge of the sedges catching insects on the water. A little while later they learn to dive for invertebrates and quickly grow in size. The female may suddenly decide one day that they have been at one particular loch long enough and she will encourage her youngsters, usually in the evening, during the pale summer night or in the early morning, to head off across country to a new destination. Some mothers will take their youngsters up to 5 miles to a big river to spend the rest of their growing-up period. Nowadays the goldeneye is one of the fastest-increasing breeding ducks that we have in Scotland. This female calling in today at our loch is just a transient visitor. I

can see that she is not in breeding condition this year, because she does not have a pale tip to her bill. Maybe she is just having a look and one day she may nest in this loch or in one nearby. She will be catching aquatic insects, like caddis-fly larvae, beetles and other underwater creatures while she dives, and soon I expect her to depart, leaving the caddis flies and beetles to the local tufted ducks.

New spring flowers appear daily — marsh marigolds grow in profusion along the water's edge (left) and on the bank (above) among the old birches is a veritable carpet of wood anemones.

SPRING

Return to the Arctic

It is one of those lovely calm evenings in the first days of May where the countryside looks new and crinkling as if just unwrapped from cellophane. There is warmness in the air and the day is winding down. An hour ago I was down on the estuary, looking out over the mud flats at low tide, the salt marsh busy with noisy redshanks. Ahead of me on the flats of the wide bay were about 6000 pink-footed geese. They were gathered in rank after rank of brown-headed, blue-grey birds. The noise was incredible; there was always a group rising, flying around and landing again. The nervousness and excitement of migration was upon them. Now, as I sit on one of the hillocks overlooking the loch, I can see the geese rising up out of the bay and heading north-westwards. Their flight path is about a mile to the north of the loch and as they set course for the Arctic they fly higher and higher into the evening skies. Some of them get cold feet at the last moment and, after flying a mile or so, swirl round and return to the bay, before starting their journey again.

At least 3000 or 4000 of the birds have headed off during the time that I have watched and I have experienced the most fantastic feeling of journeying to the Arctic. I was fortunate one summer to go to Iceland and Greenland to study pink-footed geese on their breeding grounds. Now, when I see the geese leave for their summer homes, I know exactly what lies ahead. When the furthest travellers reach the mountains of the North-east Greenland National Park, sandwiched between the ice cap and the frozen Arctic Ocean, they will find that the first snow has just melted and a green shadow lies across the hillsides. They will go back to their traditional nesting sites in jagged cliff faces along the big glacial valleys of Greenland. Their neighbours will include shaggy musk ox, Arctic foxes and the supreme predator of the geese, the white polar wolf. As dusk closes in and the sound of geese has disappeared, my thoughts continue to return to my unforgettable memories of the awe-inspiring white wolves of Greenland.

SPRING

The last arrivals

The last migrants have arrived. When I see and hear spotted flycatchers in the woods and swifts screaming overhead, I know that spring migration is over and summer is upon us. I always think of swifts as summer birds in Scotland. They are birds of our villages and it's a special day for me when I arrive at the local post office and hear the sound of screaming as the swifts rush down the middle of the village, chasing each other and choosing their mates for the summer. They nest under the eaves of the buildings, although we see them sometimes flying low over our loch, catching insects.

The birds over the loch have come from a village about 3 miles away, but some may nest closer. Occasionally swifts will nest in trees, laying their eggs in the old nest holes of great-spotted woodpeckers, which they search out by flying through open woodland identifying these distinctive holes. I remember once a pair of great-spotted woodpeckers was nesting in a dead pine tree not far from my home, where a nature photographer was filming the departure of the young woodpeckers. Slowly the whole brood of young came out and flew off into the forest nearby. Hardly had the vacant nest become cold before a pair of swifts dived in to take it over. Within a couple of days, they were laying their first eggs and successfully reared a family, thanks to the woodpeckers' wood-working skills.

Early-morning mist rises from the loch.
A newly-born roe deer fawn sleeping in a mossy bed (opposite) is
a beautiful sight. Gently breathing, the dark liquid eyes unmoving,
his inborn command is to lie still — never move! Ours
should be: look but never touch!

SUMMER

The lightest of mists is rising from the water as I walk through the leafy trees towards the loch this morning. It is very early and the birds are in full song, absolutely drowning out my thoughts as I walk along. The pungent smell of a fox assaults my nostrils as I skirt the southern edge of the loch — I don't think he is far ahead of me. There's no doubt he will have either smelt me or heard me — we humans are not blessed with the airy footfall of the red fox. He would not expect to see people walking this path so early in the morning. But I know that one of the very best times to visit a Highland loch is in the early

morning, just after dawn in late May. There is the warm feeling too of a hot sunny day in prospect. The atmosphere is almost fragile, slightly chilly in hollows, with the water very still, just broken by the ripples of the ducklings following their mothers and by the little orange-headed coot chicks dashing to meet their parents as they come up from a dive.

I sit at the far end of the loch and look back towards the rising sun, a red burning orb in the eastern sky. It is a scene of superb tranquillity; yet the powerful pulse of nature, I know, is slowly awakening to the new day. A male reed bunting sings from one of the bulrushes. His song is rather monotonous but his bold black and white head markings and his rich chestnut back make up for his mournful tune. The mute swan family are busy feeding near the island, the young looking rather spiky, uncannily like ugly ducklings as they moult from their soft down into their first greyish-white feathers. With measured steps, a roe buck walks daintily down to drink at the edge of the willows. Master of his patch, he knows that his two does have fawns tucked away in the long grasses. A newly born roe-deer fawn sleeping in a mossy bed in early summer is a most beautiful sight. It's a couple of years since I happened upon my last one, nearly treading on the youngster as I walked through knee-high bog myrtle and a carpet of white, wispy cottongrass. Below me, in absolute stillness, was a fawn, just a day or two old. Chestnut brown, fawn and black, boldly marked with white spots and blotches, the greyish black ears delicately fringed with white hairs and the black nose like wet ebony. Gently breathing, the dark liquid eyes were unmoving. His inborn instinct was to lie still – never move! I marvelled at the fawn's delicate beauty, just as I have always done when I stumble across one hidden in long vegetation. I never ever touch these youngsters, never stroke them, never speak to them, for I believe it is very important that my scent does not linger in their fur when the mother returns.

If you ever find a fawn like this, remember it is not lost: its mother knows exactly where it is. Never pick it up or touch it, and never take it away because you think it is abandoned. Its mother will return when it needs its next feed, and if she does have difficulty remembering the exact place, she will give a special gentle call and the fawn will answer with a high pitched peeping. She usually has two young and she feeds them several times a day, then hides them again. When they are stronger, they follow their mother through the woods on their incredibly long matchstick-like legs.

A female mallard swims very close to me, right at the water's edge. Her newly hatched brood are so tiny, so delicately buff and brown as they dash around in circles after tiny insects on the surface of the water. At times they jump several inches into the air to grab a tasty morsel flying overhead – delightful and entertaining little water babies. They are very difficult to count, as they scamper this way and that over the loch, but suddenly their mother gives a sharp call, a quiet urgent quack, and they immediately tumble towards her. As they assemble obediently behind her I am able to count them: there are twelve. I wonder if they are from the nest beside the path in the brambles.

It is a few moments now since the mallard went by and, unexpectedly, the still water is broken by a plop as something dives into the water. I look down with my binoculars and see a small creature swimming around under the water. It is silvery coloured and padding quite violently. I recognize the mouse-like shape as it comes to the surface: a water shrew. Water shrews are blackish above and paler below, although they look silvery underwater because of the air trapped in their fur. These animals live in wetland habitats and get their food on land, amongst the marshy vegetation or by swimming underwater to catch aquatic insects. They will eat creatures as large as a quite big juicy worm.

All three species of shrews live in this area. Common and pygmy shrews are widely spread throughout the countryside and are also found in gardens and farmland. Occasionally I have seen them rush across the path as I have walked the lochside. They are very energetic little creatures, with a hyperactive lifestyle, feeding principally on invertebrates, quite unlike rodents such as mice and voles which search out food like fruit, nuts and grain. Occasionally, when our cat brings a dead one to the back door, I get a chance to have a closer look at this little velvety creature with its long snout. The unusual musky odour from the shrew's flank glands are not to the liking of cats, so they do not eat them, instead discarding them on our doorstep. Most mammals find them repellent, but avian predators like kestrels and owls have no such misgivings.

I walk to my familiar bramble patch, which is now a well-formed bush of large bright-green leaves, a real bushy hiding place for a duck compared to the skeletal bush of April. Sure enough, the nest is empty — it has served its purpose. The duck down is already looking

OPPOSITE
The loch is now in its summer splendour.
A floating carpet of flowering bogbean fringes
the island and the shore-line trees are in full leaf.
This is a time of plenty for all creatures.
A water shrew catches its prey at the edge of
the loch (below) or when diving under the water.

worn, the dry leaves are scattered and broken eggshells litter the nest. The ducklings have hatched. There is not a single egg left complete, so this was a very successful hatch. Twelve eggs and twelve ducklings: our female mallard has done very well so far this year. I wonder how many of her ducklings will survive. Life is hard on ducklings. They can get lost or wet and chilled, be snapped from below by a marauding pike or grabbed by a stoat on the bank, or even be hunted by the merciless mink which have become established in this area after escaping from fur farms.

As I leave the loch, a male peregrine falcon flies across the top of the trees, the ducks below scattering across the water in panic; the distinctive pointed wings and powerful body of this superb aerial hunter is enough to put fear into every bird apart from the mute swans. He is clearly not that desperate, for he just nonchalantly passes over. The nearest eyrie is 5 miles or more away, and this bird needs to travel throughout his territory in order to catch enough prey. Maybe he's on his way to hunt waders on the estuary; like most male raptors, his days at this time of the season are a never-ending quest to satisfy the hunger of his growing young. He is speedily sent on his way by a pair of mobbing curlews from the marsh next door, where they have their newly hatched chicks. Curlews make no pretence about being annoyed when predators pass their territory — they give some of the noisiest mobbing reactions of any bird. Their alarm calls vary in intensity, depending on the size of threat from the potential predator. At home, my local pair of curlews, which bring their young to our hayfields after hatching them in the forest bogs nearby, give the most blood-curdling calls when they spot a fox slinking through the bog-myrtle bushes in their marshy home. The fox certainly knows he's been spotted, and so do we!

As I reach the end of my walk, I see a few scattered feathers on the path — unfortunate evidence that some bird has been killed during the night. A careful look at the feathers reveals that they belong to a female pheasant. She had probably been sitting on a nest in the scrub and long grass nearby, only to be killed by a fox which smelt her out as he searched for food during the night. After killing the pheasant, he dragged her away to his den to feed his young, the feathers obvious proof of the night-time struggle. The other day, one of the fishermen told me he had seen a fox carrying a domestic hen as he was fishing quietly on the loch early one morning; it had headed away through the woods towards the west. I expect there's an earth somewhere in the thickets of gorse and brambles that grow on the sand and gravel banks that run away westwards from the loch. The foxes have undoubtedly chosen a secluded place to rear their young and it would be difficult to find, because the ground is so broken and hard to penetrate.

Near my home there are several places where foxes have traditionally had their young; most of them are known to the local farmers, who hunt them every spring because they are worried for their lambs. Occasionally a pair of foxes will escape the dogs and the gun and rear their young in peace. Early summer is the time of year to watch the family life of the foxes; it is a most superb sight to see a family of young foxes playing at the mouth of their den. You have to be very careful with your approach: the wind must not be blowing towards the foxes or your presence will be smelt immediately by the vixen and the cubs will be led to safety below ground. It is also necessary to keep very quiet, sitting several hundred yards away from the den and watching through binoculars. It is an absolute delight to observe the young foxes playing around the den, chasing and fighting, rolling over and over, or playing tag with the remains of their prey, usually the tattered wing of a bird or the old leg of a rabbit.

If you visit the breeding den, you will find that all the grass and vegetation close to it is flattened down by their antics. Around the entrance hole is strewn the evidence of their kills: bird feathers and wings, rabbit legs and sometimes the tail of a lamb. A farmer need only see one lamb tail outside a den to say that this is a real lamb-killer, although quite often the remains come from dead lambs which the fox has scavenged rather than killed. Field voles are the favourite food of foxes and, in years when there are plenty of voles, both parents go out hunting voles once the young are larger. It's fascinating to see a fox pouncing on voles in long vegetation, its cocked ears trying to track the movements of the vole, then up on to its hind legs before pouncing like a cat into the grass.

In winter, the islands can be reached by
walking on the ice, but at other times
it's a very brave fox (right) which swims
to look for a meal. But with cubs
growing fast in the den (above),
it's a struggle to catch enough
food for them.

Summer flowers and anthills

This afternoon the woodland around the loch is alive with the high-pitched squeaking chatter of young birds. These newly fledged young are being fed by their parents, who are searching through the leaves of the trees for caterpillars while the young call incessantly for more food. But this is indeed a bounteous time. It is midsummer and food is plentiful, so the young birds and animals are growing ever faster every day. Flowers bloom in vigorous profusion. Bright purple spikes of marsh orchids gleam in a rosette of dark green leaves. The showy white bogbeans are very beautiful growing in the shallower waters of the loch. Spiky tufts of pinky-white flowers burst from the surface of the water. The coots love the flower spikes of bogbean; they peck away busily at the growing flower heads, rather disrupting the beautiful floral display that the bogbean produces in the summer. It all reminds me of a noisy playground during break, as the previously cooped-up children rush out shouting, singing and playing games.

It is hot along the woodland path, and as I reach the wood-ant nest I see that it is frantic with activity. I stop to watch them and, as always, I admire their energy and commitment. In front of my feet they cross the path in an incredibly busy file, some heading out to forage, others lugging back food to the nest. The ant motorways stretch away into the woods and the ants all seem to know what they are doing. This is a large nest, about 18 inches high and nearly 3 feet across. It is made of pine needles, small twigs, grasses and forest debris. It is swarming with brown and chestnut wood ants, and if I wave my open hand just above the nest the ants squirt formic acid at the intruder. A quick sniff of my hand reveals the pungent odour of the ants' defensive spray. There is a fair amount of activity on the anthill in the warm sunshine, almost as if doors and windows had been flung open to allow the pleasant fresh warmth to filter through the musty chambers of the anthill. In heavy rain and, of course, in winter, the hatches are battened down with a thick canopy of pine needles, leaves and sticks.

In some pinewoods these anthills can measure 2 feet 6 inches in height and are well spread through the forest. In summer thousands of wood ants can be seen travelling up and down the pine-tree trunks, carrying pine needles, resin and insects back to their nests and undoubtedly helping protect the tree from potential insect pests. The wood ant has a fascinating lifestyle – ordered and organized by the females. It isn't often that you come across a new anthill because they survive as a social community and live together in harmony without needing to set up smaller colonies. Occasionally a new nest will be established, though: after a cloud of flying ants has taken a 'nuptial flight'. This always happens on a hot summer's day and includes a winged female ant or fertile female, who takes with her all the other maiden queen ants in the nest, as opposed to infertile females or workers. At the same time, all the males take flight also; flight is essential to mating.

The biology of the queen ant enables her to take, at this one union, all the fertilizing sperm of the male and store them in a special sperm bank in her body, and to release them one by one for the fertilization of her own eggs, which she lays at the rate of one every ten minutes. This will be her job for the rest of her life, which may last anything from six to sixteen years. The male, having shot his bolt, dies. Once the eggs hatch, the female will feed the larvae on liquid from her own mouth until they pupate, which could be several months. She, meanwhile, is living off her own fat, but all this sacrifice is worthwhile because the first larvae to hatch will be of the third sex, the infertile female workers. They take on the job of feeding, nursing, housing, defending the queen, the eggs and the larvae – in short the whole ant community.

In some of the slightly drier areas at the edge of the marsh, there is a lovely carpet of water avens. I particularly like the deep wine-red flowers nestling in the dark greenish leaves, which are rather woolly looking and covered in greyish hairs. Highland lochs are also specially noted for their spectacular displays of water lilies. On quite a few lochs, the white water lily flourishes in profusion, while in a few secluded places the least yellow water lily grows. I witnessed a most beautiful scene recently at the loch near my home, where the water lilies grow close to the edge of a big mossy marsh. Roe deer love to

The coots are busy nesting around the loch and they often paddle through the rafts of bogbean pecking at the brilliant showy flowers (below).

graze there in early summer. During the middle of the day they hide in the reed beds, but they come out in the evening to walk gently across the sphagnum mosses to the edge of the loch. One evening I saw a doe dawdling along close to the edge of the water where the water lilies were growing just by her feet. Close behind her was the most perfect pair of fawns in their lovely white-spotted juvenile coats. The roe-deer family and the water lilies against the mirror-like black water were sensational in the soft velvet light of evening.

Sadly, in recent years we have had a few people coming up from the south to steal water lilies from Highland lochs for sale at garden centres. It is illegal to take these beautiful plants from the wild, as they are protected by the Wildlife and Countryside Act. Fortunately, several groups of these marauders have recently been caught and prosecuted in Highland courts. I think water lilies are there for people to enjoy, whether they live locally or come on holiday, and certainly not to be torn out by their roots from the bottom of our lochs and transplanted to plastic-lined urban ponds in the polluted atmosphere of our cities.

From my viewpoint at the south side of the loch, I look away towards the Black Isle and the sea cliffs of Cromarty. Apart from the blue of the sky and the varied greens of wood and field, the most obvious colour is a brilliant rich yellow. The showy banks of broom and gorse are a spectacular feature of the Moray Firth plain, and today they blaze in golden splendour. The greatest displays of colour follow gravel banks and ridges left millennia ago by the retreating ice. All around the air is laden with the warm, heavy perfume of summer. As I turn, I glance through the open birch woodland with its newly growing fronds of bracken which are slowly obscuring the meadow of bluebells that has cheered me during the last month. I ponder these sweeping floral displays of yellow and blue, and compare them to the subtle flowers which bloom shyly in sheltered places beside the loch, each flower a gem in its own right.

The delicate and widespread chickweed wintergreen is a special favourite. Its six- or seven-petalled white flower sits atop a spindly stem set with a whorl of pale green lanceolate leaves; the orange-tipped stamens complete the picture. It is a small plant, about 4 inches high, from whence it gets its scientific name, *Trientalis* (third of a foot). In a few favoured localities in the ancient pines, two other similarly beautiful and individual flowers grow on the forest floor. The delicate twin flower throws up its flower stem from trailing plants which grow among the moss on old pine stumps in the woods. This rare plant, with two pale pinky-white hanging trumpets on each flower stem, has a gentle fragrance and long ago was the special favourite of the famous Swedish botanist Carl von Linné, who named this plant after himself, *Linnaeus borealis*. In a few very special places the graceful one-flowered wintergreen blooms; its single white- and green-tinged nodding flower gives the plant its other name, St Olav's candlestick.

The osprey legend

When I was at the loch today, I heard a noisy splash as I was kneeling down looking at an intricate spider's web hanging from a dark green juniper bush. I knew there was only one bird capable of making a splash like that, so I ran quickly to a clearing in the trees where I had a wide view of the loch. The osprey was just on the point of rising up out of the rippled water, shaking the water off its plumage, straining to gain height on its desperately flapping wings, its talons empty. It soared upwards, flapping furiously, and then stopped briefly to shake its whole body and head in one long, wriggling movement, rather like a dog shaking itself after it has been swimming. Having shed most of the water, it gained height more easily, until it was about 100 feet above the loch, continuing its ceaseless search for an unwary fish. Soaring on broad wings, occasionally hovering, it carefully searched the waters below.

I could see the bird most wonderfully and, because I was hidden under a shady oak tree, it did not see me. It stooped, it hovered, it checked, it thought it could see another fish, but no, it did not get the right view, or maybe the fish moved at the last moment. The osprey gained height again and continued to search the loch from end to end, moving effortlessly on its 5-foot wing span and swivelling its brilliant, piercing yellow eyes for the slightest flicker of a trout in the dark waters. I could see it was a male bird, as the males are paler

Water avens backlit by the setting sun over the loch.

OPPOSITE ABOVE
*In marshy places the distinctive flowers and
leaves of the butterwort grow in profusion.*

OPPOSITE
*Nearby in a few special places in the ancient
pine woods, the delicate twin flower trails
over the forest floor.*

on the breast, whiter on the head and have distinctively paler patches on the side of the beautifully patterned brown and white marked tails, as well as being smaller than the bulkier females. This was almost certainly the male from the nearest nest, which is not many miles away, but he was not having any luck on this particular evening. After another few circuits of the loch, he set off purposefully towards the firth: if the tide had just turned, he'd surely catch a flatfish.

Nowadays fishing can be easier on the estuary than it is on some of the inland lochs. Of course, there are days when the pike are moving into the sunny shallows to spawn or to sunbathe and they make easy prey and good eating for ospreys. At other times the trout are rising to the surface to catch flies and once again the ospreys home in on these as a ready supply of food. But if freshwater fish are proving difficult to catch, the birds always know they can catch flatfish. Or rather, they are nearly always successful in catching flatfish unless there is a thick fog coming in off the sea or high winds are churning the shallow water. There is no fog this evening, the tide has turned and the salt water is trawling back in over the sand flats, a snaky line of foam relentlessly pushing towards the shore. The flounders, locally called flukes, will be following the incoming tide; every few minutes they dash a few yards towards the shore, searching for worms that are wriggling to the surface of the recently flooded sand. Flatfish make a distinctive little sandy cloud, as they hide themselves in the sandy bottom. Ospreys recognize these puffs of sand: with a rapid dive they hit the surface of the water and bring up the flounders from the shallow bed of the estuary, then set off back towards their nests. I always marvel at their skill; how clever to snatch a fluke from a foot of water yet not damage themselves by hitting the sea bed.

At the moment, this male osprey has a mate at home who has just hatched three chicks in the great eyrie in the tree top. The female's job is to tend and protect the young from the elements and predators while her mate's main task is hunting. Fishing has now become a very serious business, whereas during the incubation period he needed to catch only one decent-sized fish a day. He would eat the front half of the fish and then offer the second half to his mate.

While she had a break from incubating and ate her fill, he sat on the eggs. Now he has to catch three or four fish a day, and soon it will rise to six or even seven a day, when the chicks are at their most hungry and growing fastest. He will provide fresh fish right through to the end of July, when the young will be ready to fly. Then they will follow their parents to the waters to practise hunting, knowing that if they fail they will always be fed. After a few weeks they will become classy fishermen and, once they are capable of feeding themselves, the male can relax. The young may learn to catch fish on this particular loch, but more likely they will go to the estuary to fish there. Then they are on their own and before them lies their first long and dangerous migration to the osprey's ancestral winter quarters in West Africa.

The return of the osprey to Scotland is a very well-known story. Briefly, the first pair came back to nest in the 1950s after an absence of half a century. Those first pioneers found the lochs and forests of Strathspey to their liking, being very similar to their original homes in Norway and Sweden, so it was not surprising that they chose to nest beside Loch Garten in an old pine set amongst the ancient Caledonian forest. Ever since then a pair of ospreys has nested there. The Loch Garten ospreys have become world famous and the local village, Boat of Garten, has been named the Osprey Village.

In those early years, the RSPB carefully guarded the new colonists, which allowed them to nest successfully and rear Scottish-bred young. As more young were reared, some of them returned to Scotland to nest and to increase the population. Following the first pair in the 1950s, we found a second pair of ospreys nesting in Strathspey in 1963. Numbers increased to three pairs in 1966 and then nearly annually until there were fourteen pairs in 1973. By this time at least twenty-one youngsters had been reared in Scotland. We now know that about 30–40 per cent of the young ospreys that are reared in Scotland actually survive their juvenile years in Africa and southern Europe. They return to Scotland for the first time when they are just two years old, but it may not be until they are three or four years old that they will actually breed. The young prefer to come back and nest very close to where they were reared. This may mean building a

RIGHT
The osprey is now well spread in Scotland with over 80 pairs living in large tree-top eyries. The pair nearest the loch have three large young (below) and the male bird occasionally hunts over our loch on his fishing forays.

new nest or occupying a place at an established eyrie. However, the population does not spread very quickly. Instead there is a gradual build-up of numbers in different localities before they move out to establish new nesting areas. Sometimes we help the dispersion by providing artificial osprey nests in new areas; over the years this conservation work has been very successful in helping the population to spread and increase. Nowadays the nests we build in high trees are near enough indistinguishable from the real thing.

Once the number of youngsters being reared each summer started to increase, the population also rose more steadily. By 1977 there were twenty pairs, by 1982 thirty pairs, by 1986 forty-three pairs and in 1992 we found seventy-six pairs of ospreys nesting in Scotland. That year saw two other landmarks as well. One was that the number of young reared in a single year in Scotland passed the 100 mark, with at least 101 youngsters fledged from Scottish nests. It was also interesting that the cumulative total of young ospreys which had been reared in Scotland since 1954 passed the 1000 mark. So the situation for ospreys is looking better all the time. They were once a common bird throughout the whole of the British Isles, nesting beside lakes and rivers and on the sea coast as long as there was suitable fishing. From the Middle Ages, man started to put pressure on ospreys and they were finally exterminated in the early years of this century. Thank goodness they have had another chance and are now slowly returning.

The osprey I saw today is nesting in a big Scots pine, where there has been a pair of ospreys for eleven years. Near to it are several other pairs which have started to nest more recently as the population has continued to grow. This bird has three chicks. I was at the nest not long ago, when they were just a few weeks old and still rather reptilian in character, although the grey-white down was starting to give way to the first brownish feathers. I estimate this pair will have their young flying by the third week of July.

About the end of the first week of July I will return to the nest with one of my colleagues who will climb the tree and lower the young carefully to the ground so that I can ring them. I hope we will find three youngsters there, as this is usually a successful nest;

over the years I have ringed a total of twenty-three young at this nest. Since the ringing programme began, about 700 young ospreys have been ringed in Scotland and we have received reports of these birds from West Africa south to Guinea, as well as on migration through France and Iberia, with stragglers as far east as Yugoslavia and, surprisingly, as far north as Iceland. Nowadays more reports come from sightings of the colour rings placed on the young birds, including very interesting information on old faithfuls which nest in the same eyrie year after year. My oldest pair is a twenty-year-old male and an eighteen-year-old female which have reared a total of twenty-five young in their lifetime together.

Our bird hunts on other freshwater lochs, similar to this one, as well as in the firth, so difficulties in catching fish can arise from different circumstances. Only two years ago, we had a period of very bad foggy weather in June. We call the fog that comes in from the North Sea on an easterly wind 'the haar'. It is dense and cold and quiet, and it can last for days or even weeks. In those conditions it is impossible for the ospreys to see the surface of the sea and they find it very difficult to catch enough food for their young. That summer when we went to the eyrie to ring the young we found only one live chick; the other two were dead in the nest through lack of food. This year it looks better and I expect our pair to rear all three young.

Hay-making in the Highlands

The woodland is alive with newly fledged young birds. The trees around the loch are crawling with young warblers and tits, the bulrushes resound to the scolding of a family of wrens. When I look closely, the leaves are covered in green caterpillars and food is extremely plentiful. The parent birds are trying their best to raise the largest possible brood of young. They know they can have bad years when it is very cold and wet during late May or June and caterpillars are very scarce; in those years most young birds die. In fact, cold wet weather is a real killer for young songbirds and visits to nest boxes will reveal brood after brood of dead nestlings. Nature can seem cruel at times, but adult birds know that if it becomes

The most dominant residents of the loch
are a pair of mute swans (right) which
return each spring to raise a family.
The female takes her tiny cygnets
(above) for a swim across the lake.

extremely difficult to find food, then there is no choice. Youngsters die so that the adults can live for another day when they can lay new clutches of eggs and rear broods of young in more conducive circumstances.

The loch itself is home to a host of young birds — goodness knows how many young mallard are paddling around with their mothers. They are now well feathered and gaining in size. The tufted duck family have six small young, as they are quite late nesters. They are busy diving in the shallows, disturbing the turbid water with its dusty film of pollen. The coots have two broods; the older chicks are now independent, but the later ones have only just hatched and are still demanding to be fed. The dabchicks haven't done well. They have just one surviving chick, but a little display the other day suggests that they may try for a late brood. The swan family dominates the scene. The cygnets are now half grown; they already know the feed-time routine up at the boat house. This is a time of plenty for them.

Long, lazy summer days — very long days indeed, for on 21 June in the north of Scotland it hardly seems to get dark at all. It is certainly still light at 11 p.m., and if you stay up all night you will find that the sun is already rising at 1.30 or so in the morning. I used to live in the Shetland Isles, several hundred miles further north, and there the sun just sank briefly below the horizon in the middle of Midsummer's Night.

Once Midsummer's Day is past, the farmers on the crofts and farms above the loch are thinking of hay-making. They are waiting for a forecast of a long settled period of fine weather, with a good chance that it is going to be hot and sunny, with no rain. By this time, the grass has grown well, rich and lush, maybe with wild plants starting to flower in some of these meadows. Now is the time to cut the hay before the grass goes to seed.

There is a sudden rush of activity: the whine of hay-mowers going round and round the fields cutting the grass in lovely sappy swathes. How different to days long gone when these same fields would have echoed to the talk of men as they swung their scythes, with occasional breaks to hone the steel with the rasping noise of a stone. This is a dangerous time for the frogs and toads which headed into the long grass after the mating season's activities in the loch in the spring. The act of hay-cutting is a very serious disruption to their lives, as well as to the small rodents and large insects that live in the grass fields. But for the other animals and birds that hunt these creatures, this is a sudden bonanza and, as you see the tractors travel around the field leaving their green tramlines of freshly cut hay expertly laid down in long lines, the jackdaws and rooks converge on the fields. Along with other birds, they search for creatures that have been disturbed. Obviously they do well from eating the odd frog or big insect, or maybe even a mouse, for they seem to know the noise of the mower and it draws them to the fields. Sometimes even rabbits are killed by the mowers and are then scavenged by the crows. When we cut our hayfields we always keep a sharp eye open for young roe deer which have been hidden in the fields by their mothers, and we make certain that they are chased out before cutting begins.

Hay-making is a tense time for farmers, who hope that the sun will dry up and wither the grass very quickly. In fact, quickly-made hay is by far the best. When it starts to dry, and if it dries quickly and is green, then it is really good, it is turned several times to achieve this degree of dryness and is finally gathered into rows and baled. There is no more satisfying sight than a barn filled with freshly baled, sweet-smelling hay and the fields successfully harvested of a superb hay crop. Once that is done, the farmers of the Highlands are very satisfied indeed; there is nothing like having your winter feed secured safely in the barn. This is always a period of intense hard work in the Highlands, but as long as it goes successfully it is a period of great contentment. I won't forget the summer of 1985 when we tried and failed to make hay and were still dismally turning a useless crop in late September. It rained every day that summer.

OVERLEAF
*Early summer: the loch reflects
the blue of the sky, but there is
still snow on the distant
mountain peaks.*

Often, in the past, there would be celebrations as the last of the hay was brought in from the fields. On our own croft, my wife can remember that on the evening when the last hay was brought in there was always a fiddler or two ready to play a tune. No matter how tired they were — and hay-making is very tiring work — they would dance the Hay-Makers Jig on the green at the end of the croft house. Sometimes a piper would be there as well to celebrate the successful hay harvest.

Another lovely memory I have is of when we stayed one summer with friends on a farm among the forests of Sweden. There we helped with the hay-making, working to get the last of the hay into the great big red wooden barn, typical of a Swedish farm. As the day arrived when the final crop was being gathered, the old granny of the family and some of the younger children went off into the forest to gather wild strawberries. That evening we had a special celebration dinner and the crowning moment was when granny brought in the special hay-making cake. It was the lightest of sponges, topped with a layer of cream and then a layer of wild strawberries, a layer of cream, a layer of wild strawberries, a layer of cream and finally wild strawberries. Everyone had a slice of this special treat, which is made only on the day that the hay is successfully stored in the barn.

One bird that we sometimes hear at this time of the year is the quail. I listened in vain for them the other evening as I sat beside the loch. A few days earlier, in another part of the area, I heard the call of a quail coming from a cornfield as I walked along the sea wall with the salt marsh on my left and the farm fields on my right. The quail is a small partridge-like bird which migrates to Scotland from the Mediterranean; a few pairs nest in our district in the very best of summers. They have a lovely call, rather ventriloquial in nature, which sounds like 'wet my lips, wet my lips', repeated over and over again. Once you have heard it and once you have read the description of the call in words, you cannot get the 'tune' out of your mind.

That evening, while straining my ears for quail above the chatter and buzz of normal lochside noise, I heard an eerie squeaking call in the dusk which I recognized immediately. The call was slow and occasionally repeated; at a distance it sounded just like an iron gate squeaking on its hinge. I left the path and quietly stalked the noise through the pine wood. In the bough of a large pine, overlooking an open forest bog of stunted trees and sphagnum mosses, I found the performers. Two young long-eared owls blinked down at me, silent now that I had found them. They were two-thirds grown, still covered in brownish-grey down but with their feathers growing fast. Like their parents, they had tufts on top of their heads, in their case greyish tufts of down rather than feathers, and only for decoration rather than for hearing. Their orange eyes glowered at me and I was struck again by the precociousness of young long-eared owls. They leave their nests well before they can properly fly and scramble through the nearby trees, calling frequently from dusk to dawn so that their parents know where to deliver the nightly supply of voles and mice.

Fishing in the rain

There are two people fishing today on the loch in a small boat and the ducks are keeping a good distance from them. The wildfowl like people arriving with food and will come very close to the bank, but people in boats waving fishing rods are another matter and they keep well clear. They will spend an hour or two trying to catch trout, although at times the rain showers are so heavy that I believe they will give up unless the fishing is good. In summer the lochs are well visited by fishermen; in fact, a day at the trout in a remote loch, miles from the road, is the very best of sport. People have always been associated with water; in the past it was more often used for transport and further back still people lived in close harmony with Highland lochs. Islands in some lochs have been shown to be artificial and made of wood and rock. They are called 'crannogs' and were used for habitation in times when life was far more hazardous and a water barrier was important for safety.

The woodland path is so wet that it is slippery walking in places, but there is that special smell of freshly soaked earth. A gauzy mist hangs just above the gloomy pines, and birch leaves hang despondently as the rain drips from their branches. Only the alder appears buoyant, its green leathery leaves polished by the summer downpour and its roots invisibly

*On summer evenings, the eerie squeaking call
of young long-eared owls can be heard in the woods
near the loch. The adults are hunting voles
well before dusk on the short summer nights
of the Scottish Highlands.*

and greedily sucking up the moisture. The alder has to have its feet in water; in days gone by its wood was much sought after for buildings which stood in water. In Venice, one of the most famous bridges, the Rialto, is built on piles or great posts of alder wood driven deep into the bed of the canal. It was also used in early times for making boats but is of no use for fenceposts or gates as it decays quite quickly in dry soil. When I have to cut up an alder tree which has perhaps fallen over a fence or blown down, I notice particularly that the chips which fall below my chain saw are white, but once exposed to daylight, just like a banana, they change colour and become reddish pink.

Although the trees and flowers dismally hang their heads during this deluge, it will eventually benefit them, giving a boost to the sap and an added fragrance to the flowers. The vibrant contrasting colours of a cluster of butterworts in the marsh are enhanced by the little crystal droplets running down the star-shaped rosette of lime-green leaves, above which is a deep purple-blue flower of tremendous clarity. Our cows love this bog violet, as it is sometimes called, and it is believed that the milk of a cow which has eaten butterwort will protect newborn babies. Cheek by jowl with the butterwort is the ungraciously named lousewort, with its fresh pretty pink snapdragon flowers. The old people used to say this plant gave lice and liverworms to cattle. I should think the cows know that too and don't eat the lousewort.

The intricately woven spiders' webs of yesterday are now glittering nets of moisture and are no longer efficient fly traps. The spiders have work to do once the rain has dried. The smell of moist earth is all pervading, as I walk along the lochside; somehow it is bounteous, positive and hopeful. All at once my feet feel hot and heavy in this moist, lush atmosphere and I have the urge to walk barefoot to feel the soaking earth beneath my feet, to enjoy the dewy wash of warm summer rain. Today there is no smalltalk from the woodland birds, there is a silence, a very acceptable silence, all around the loch. But there is a music in the soft air, a gentle patter of raindrops on the loch's black surface, a rustle of droplets from leaf to leaf, with as yet no wind in the tree tops to increase the pitch. I listen and watch enchanted, and the rain drips, drips, drips from the leaves.

SUMMER

Dragonflies and rain geese

It was one of those lovely evenings and I just sat and watched the life of the loch. There was a hum of insects everywhere. The wretched midges were being a bit of a nuisance and it was hard not to respond by scratching. As soon as a mosquito tried to land on me, I got out the mosquito oil. In times past, people use to scrunch up bog-myrtle leaves and rub them on to their faces to try to keep off the mosquitoes. Close to the loch there were also far too many flies; in fact, the peace of the evening was nearly spoilt by the numbers of insects that landed on me. But some of the insects are beautiful and the most attractive of all are the dragonflies. Dragonflies are just so sensationally coloured: some are electric blue, others are brilliantly patterned green and black, and others are reddish brown. In some

*The loch is home to many dragonflies. This common
hawker rests beside the water's edge. Below the
surface (opposite), a pike glides through the shallows.*

species the male is blue and the female is reddish brown, so that
when they mate they fly around, joined head to tail, as incredible
double-winged insects of two contrastingly brilliant colours. They
have lovely names as well: fourspot chasers and common hawkers,
blue damselflies, large red damselflies and white-faced darters. This
loch is a good place for dragonflies, but I don't know the names of
all the species – I just enjoy looking at them and appreciating their
beauty. All through the summer they quarter the loch and surrounding woodland, catching insects up to the size of small moths.
At other times I see the nymphs crawling out of the water on stems
of vegetation and slowly changing from a rather unattractive grub
into the most beautiful of winged insects.

Looking towards the north-west, the sun is sinking fast into the
most beautiful clear evening sky. It is so warm, such a comfortable
feeling, that I can hardly believe it when I hear the cry of the rain
goose or red-throated diver. In flight, the call is a distinctive goose-
like call, 'ga-ga-gag', of varying length, often uttered when the bird is
very high in the sky. In Scotland, this call gives the bird its local
name of rain goose, with the call signifying the coming of rain –
which is not that unlikely in Scotland! There will be no rain this
evening, or tonight, or tomorrow, as we are in a very settled spell of

weather, so the rain goose calling to his mate on the hill lochs high above me has got the forecast wrong this time. He will never land on this loch, as it is totally unsuitable for red-throated divers. This evening he is off to the Moray Firth, where he will catch sand eels to carry back to his breeding loch to feed his young.

Red-throated divers nest on small lochans on the wide-open peaty moors and this bird is probably from a nesting loch I know, about 4 miles away up on the heathery hill to the north and about 1500 feet above sea level. It is quite a tiny loch, only 30 yards across. The surrounding vegetation is rather floating, dominated by red and green sphagnum moss, and on one little island of sphagnum moss, in a corner of the loch, the divers make their nest. They crawl up and make a flat little hollow nest, where they lay two eggs. They catch nothing at all at their loch and have to fly 10 miles or more to sea to find food. They sometimes go to larger freshwater lochs, where they can catch a few trout or minnows to take to their young, but most of the food for this pair of birds is from the sea. As their young grow, the pair make return trips backwards and forwards throughout the day to bring back sand eels or other sea fish for the young divers.

The red-throated diver is doing quite well in Scotland and the population is increasing. As a result, the birds are moving further south to breed. It is found as a breeding bird throughout the north of Scotland, where it breeds mainly on moorland lochs and lochans; its strongholds are in the Highlands, the Western Isles, Orkney and Shetland, with smaller numbers south to Argyll. The population is believed to be between 1200 and 1500 pairs, with about half of them breeding in Shetland. This is one of the most easterly pairs nesting in Scotland and they have reared young in most of the years that I have known of them.

Their larger cousin, the black-throated diver, is a different bird in many ways. It nests on the large lochs of the Scottish Highlands, mainly on the western side, but a few pairs do nest in eastern lochs. They choose to breed on the larger lochs in the valleys, which often have big islands, sometimes covered with trees. The loch must also have a rich supply of fish, for the black-throated divers catch all their food on the main loch where they nest. About 150 pairs of black-throated divers breed in the Scottish Highlands, principally in Sutherland, Wester Ross and the Western Isles, with lesser numbers elsewhere in the Highland Region, northern Perthshire and Argyll. Occasional pairs have nested southwards to Dumfries and Galloway, but the species has shown a decline in this century. It is now a rare bird and in the last few decades it has not been doing very well at all. Sadly, people still steal their eggs and it is a real tragedy to find so many nests robbed each spring. Others lose their nests due to changes in water level, either flooded out by heavy rain or left high and dry by droughts when they can no longer clamber on to their nests. The future for the black-throated diver appeared so bleak, with many nests being flooded and destroyed, that the RSPB started a special conservation programme to support and protect them.

We talked to as many people as possible who owned or fished lochs which held divers in order to give better protection to these birds during the time they had eggs and nests. A programme of building and floating out artificial islands was started by the RSPB and the Forestry Commission, so that the birds could nest successfully on lochs which had severely fluctuating water levels. Initial attempts to encourage black-throated and red-throated divers to use floating islands were made in Argyll in the 1970s, but it was not until the late 1980s that a major programme of artificial nesting islands for black-throated divers was initiated. Successful use soon followed and now over fifty islands are available to divers in the Highlands. Pairs which had been flooded out year after year are now able to rear young, and other lochs, where pairs no longer attempted to breed, have been recolonized.

There were tigers beside the loch today, but they were only beetles. The path was hot, the pine needles so dry they were slippery, and every few steps on my walk brilliantly coloured tiger beetles dashed from my feet. These iridescent, greeny-blue beetles are swift at running on their six long hairy legs and at times some of them flew out of my way. They are marked by yellow spots and stripes, hence their name, and have eight eyes. Their local name is field shiner. They are harmless to us but powerful predators in the insect world, catching smaller creatures for their food.

SUMMER

Some species of tiger beetles have a most bizarre way of feeding when they are in the larval stage of their life. When the larva hatches from the egg, it digs itself a vertical hole below the surface of the ground. When the hole is complete, the young tiger-beetle larva climbs to the top of the hole and seals the entrance with its flat head, retaining its position against the wall of the hole with the aid of

The early-morning sun catches the loch: it's going to be a hot day and the loch resounds to the chatter of birds and the buzzing of insects. On the lochside path, bright green tiger beetles (above) bask in the hot sun and wait to catch their prey, in this case, a green caterpillar.

hooks on its back. In this position it waits for its prey, which consists of any small ant-like creature which may inadvertently walk over its head. As soon as this happens, the trap door, formed by the beetle's head, opens and the creature is dragged into the pit and eaten. What amazing grisly slaughter is going on all around us, without us ever noticing.

Butterflies and berries

July sees the nights slowly gaining in length, and for most birds and animals the main season of producing young is over. The young are growing and becoming independent of the adults in many species. The young ospreys are fledging on their nests and some have already flown for the first time. Many birds are already beginning to think about the shortening days of autumn. The first of the lapwings and the oystercatchers have left the fields and headed towards the coast, ready for their southwards migrations. The flowers are seeding and everywhere there is that rich feeling of the ripening of seeds and berries. The wild raspberries are red and juicy and the blaeberries are starting to swell in the forest.

This is the best month for butterflies and I noticed, as I walked by, that the clump of thistles growing close to where I normally park my car was in full flower and three small tortoiseshell butterflies were sipping nectar. A few days ago, a clouded yellow fluttered northwards across the island on the loch. It has been a very good year for this long-distance migrant butterfly, which only reaches these northern areas in the sunniest of summers. The red admirals have also been visiting the thistles and in the evening I see moths fluttering over the flowery patch as I leave for home.

In early August there is a tremendous harvest of blaeberries in some of our pine woods. Many birds feed on the blaeberries, from the smallest finches to the largest capercaillie, and also a whole variety of mammals, from mice to pine martens and foxes. In fact, 1000 years or more ago, when brown bears lived in these very woods, they would also have been feeding on blaeberries at this time of the year. The next bonanza of fruit is the wild cherries, or geans, and by mid-August the black cherries are ready, providing another harvest of fruit for wildlife and also for ourselves. I like to climb into a great big gean tree at least once each summer to gorge myself on black Highland cherries; there are far too many stones really, but the delicious taste of wild cherries is something not to be missed.

Then one day, looking up, I see the swifts flying south. Today is one of those days: a day when you sense rather than see a metamorphosis. The loch is still and heavy in the mid-afternoon sun, and there is a rumble of thunder in the distance. It is a hot afternoon, the clouds are brassy, boiling and ominous. I see lightning flash over the hill 3 or 4 miles away, a spectacular blue flash as it seeks the ground. The roar of thunder crashes towards me across the loch and I hurry for shelter in my car, otherwise I will be soaked in no time at all. I hear screaming above me and as I look up I see a closely packed flock of swifts, house martins and swallows swirling in a tight flock above my head, maybe 400 or 500 feet up in the sky. Quite often at this time in the summer you will see a flock of swifts and martins swirling in the sky, catching insects ahead of a thunderstorm. Then one day the swifts are no longer here: they have gone on their long journey to Africa. Their summer in Scotland is over. By the end of August nearly all the swifts have left, the cuckoos have gone and the warblers are getting ready to leave. The loch itself is starting to adjust to a new season — gone are the summer residents, arriving soon will be the autumn visitors from northern lands. And the loch in autumn will look different but will, as ever, be a haven of rest for some and a provider of food for others.

The autumn colours in the Scottish Highlands can
be very beautiful and a birch tree
overhanging the loch captures that beauty.

OPPOSITE
A blue tit forages in the autumn leaves.

AUTUMN

'Wink, wink, wink-wink': the excited high-pitched calling of pink-footed geese. To me, they bring the first real sound and sight of autumn. I look skywards and there, high, high up in the northern skies above the loch, are two tiny skeins of geese flying south. They are at a tremendous height, hardly visible in the blue September sky. Every now and then they give a burst of calling 'wink, wink' to keep in contact or to locate fellow travellers as they continue southwards on their migration over miles of trackless skies. This flock left Iceland this morning, 16 September, setting course over

the grey Arctic seas for Scotland and taking advantage of the fresh northerly winds which followed the depression that went through yesterday. So often in autumn, as a succession of depressions or low-pressure patterns blow in from the Atlantic Ocean, we get a fine day with strong north-west winds following a spell of rain and wind. Then we see the geese coming south after their breeding season in Iceland. There the brief Arctic summer is over, the sun hangs lower in the southern skies each day and it grows dark very quickly; the temperature drops and the cold intensifies, the need for food increases. Departure cannot be delayed; hunger must be faced. The inherent urge to migrate is overwhelming and evacuation takes place.

Some of these pink-feet will have travelled this way many times; in fact, the oldest one ringed and recovered in Scotland was over twenty-one years in age and had crossed the ocean more than forty times. They really know the route from their breeding grounds in the mountains of Iceland and Greenland to their wintering grounds in the comparatively softer Scotland. They will have departed from the southern shores of Iceland this morning and flown non-stop the 400 miles or so across the North Atlantic to the most north-westerly part of Sutherland in as little as eight hours. The old birds in the flock will easily recognize landmarks like the white tower of the lighthouse at Cape Wrath and the great sea cliffs of Clo Mor in the very north-west corner of the Scottish mainland. From there they will strike south-eastwards across the vast empty moors and scree-covered mountains of Sutherland and Ross-shire towards the fertile farmlands of Easter Ross and the Moray Firth, with their abundance of stubble fields and spilt barley. At this time of the year, however, the pink-footed geese do not linger here, except for a rest in bad weather, but continue southwards on their journey to central Scotland.

I notice that the mute swans and their young on the loch glance up inquiringly when the geese are directly overhead. The young swans have never seen such a sight before. They stretch their necks upwards, tilting their heads from side to side as they recognize the calls of kindred spirits. Maybe they wish they could fly with such power and precision as these Arctic pioneers. But never in their lives will they fly at such heights nor travel such great distances across the grey waters of northern oceans. So far these cygnets have only skimmed the water from one end of the loch to the other. Later, when their flying training has progressed, they will be ready to commute to the estuary. However, most mute swans in this area probably range no more than 30 miles from their birthplace in their whole life. Even now, after more than thirty years' birdwatching in this area, it is something of an event to see a mute swan fly at any real height or for any distance. Their close relatives the whooper swans, on the other hand, are accomplished and adventurous travellers.

As I watch these pink-footed geese moving across the dusky pink evening sky, I see the skeins changing shape, but always a larger bird is in the forefront of each V formation, with each bird a set distance behind and to the side of the goose in front. The leaders are the older birds that know the way ahead from instinct and experience. The geese are almost in silhouette: the sky is lit up by a sinking sun behind low puffs of dove-grey clouds. Because of the height at which they are flying, they take a long time to travel across the sky and I have time to count them. There are over 120. From such a height, and on such a clear and beautiful evening, the older birds can easily follow the route they know so well, southwards over the great round-shouldered Cairngorm mountains, with everlasting snow in the high corries; they will soon be able to settle back and start their long glide to earth towards Loch Leven. This superb wildfowl loch, south of the city of Perth, is a great mecca for pink-feet in the autumn.

By the time of the autumnal equinox, many of the Iceland and Greenland pink-footed geese will have reached Scotland. When I first started to watch them in this area in the early 1960s there were fewer than 50 000 wintering in Scotland each year; now there are nearly

---

OVERLEAF
*'Wink, wink, wink-wink'. The excited high-pitched
calling of a flock of pink-footed geese migrating
from Iceland to Scotland are, to me, the first real
sight and sound of autumn.*

200 000 coming south every autumn. Some geese have much more difficult migrations than others because of weather changes on their long overseas flights. Despite their experience and navigational abilities, they can get lost and find it a struggle to make landfall. But in times of good weather, and especially when the skies are clear and the wind is from the north, their journey time from Iceland can be very fast and they may even complete the first leg to the Scottish mainland in something under eight hours.

Wild whooper swans fly the same route from Iceland, also at great heights. I remember a day such as this some years ago when I was perched on a hillside overlooking a small loch by the shores of the Dornoch firth. A scattering of busily domestic mute swans, along with tufted ducks and coots, was feeding across the shallow waters of the loch; it was a calm, peaceful, late-summer scene, the still water dotted with delicately floating white swan feathers discarded by the moulting adults. Suddenly, I could hear the distant but penetrating trumpeting of whooper swans. I searched the skies, but saw nothing until a glint of white showed the presence of a flock of swans spiralling out of the sky. When first I saw them, they were still 4000 feet above sea level and were in a rapid descent. It was several minutes before they swept down to land on the loch amidst an exuberant clamour of trumpetings, and hasty retreats and complaints by the local residents. An aircraft pilot once saw some whooper swans flying at nearly 20 000 feet between Scotland and Iceland. There were seventeen whooper swans in the flock I saw that day, all adults, which was not surprising as the first travellers are usually birds which have not bred successfully that year, while families with young arrive in October. The reason I remember them so well is that with them was a smaller Bewick's swan, the wild swan found more often in Europe and southern England than in the north of Scotland. This poor bird must have got lost and travelled north to Iceland for the summer with the larger whooper swans, instead of flying eastwards to breed in Arctic Russia.

It is half an hour since the geese flew over and the sun has almost dipped behind the mountains. The loch is still busy, there is still the warmth of summer and still the hum of insects. It is a bustling summer scene as the swallows and martins chase flies across the smooth surface of the loch, but they are not here just to catch food: they are gathering together for their communal night-time roost. Before leaving Scotland in August and September for their long journey to winter in Africa, swallows, sand and house martins join together at dusk to roost in reed beds beside lochs. Sometimes the roosts are very large indeed and may involve hundreds of birds, but at our loch there is just a small reed bed, so usually only about 100 birds are to be found.

Before going to roost they spend their time swirling around above the loch, chittering happily away in noisy chasing parties. Sometimes they fly down and land in the reeds, or pretend to land and then flutter up again and skittishly swirl around once more. As darkness approaches, they become subdued and soon settle down for the night, perched on the reed stems above the water. Pied wagtails also come to the roost. First one and then another and then a couple more drop on to the reeds amongst the swallows. Surprisingly, they find each other acceptable bedfellows and there is little or no argument about who sleeps at the top or the bottom of the reed. These are the local birds that have nested in busy farmyards or in stone dykes along roadsides in the Highlands. It has been a successful breeding season and there are good numbers flitting across the loch. They will roost here for several days, or even weeks, before heading off south to spend their winter in the home counties of England.

As the evening darkens more and more birds settle in quietly for the night in the roost, late arrivals only too glad of a reedy foothold for the night. Finally, a few reed buntings come flicking across the loch, confidently landing on the bulrushes on the edge of the island before also slipping into the roost. The heavy blanket of warm summer darkness has descended and the loch is quiet; it is hard to believe that several hundred small birds are roosting in the tranquil reed bed on the other side.

Slowly, the night shift takes over; it is as though a few swallows are back on the wing. The Daubenton's bats are out in force this evening. At times they fly so close to the water that they seem to kiss their reflections as they take aquatic insects from the very surface

The swallows hawking the
loch at dusk give way to
the nightly arrival of bats.
A Daubenton's bat flies
close to the water surface after
insects, at times they seem
to kiss their reflections in
the still water.

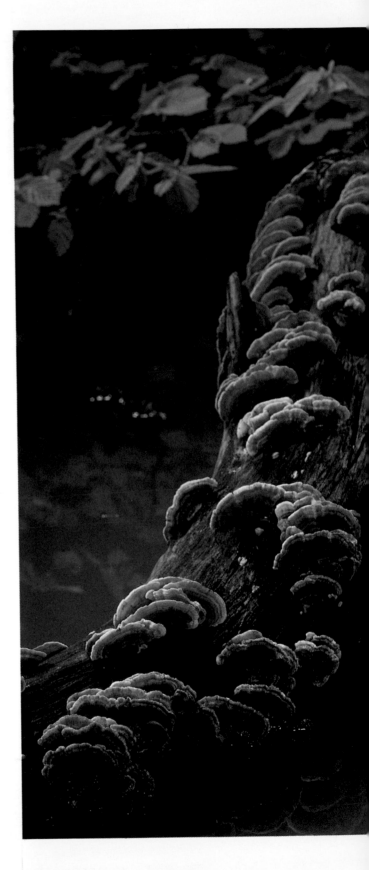

of the water or slip down to drink on the wing. There are at least six of them patrolling the loch this evening. This is the real water bat of Scotland, the one that is occasionally caught on the fly of a fisherman trying for a late fish in the gloaming. They roost nearby in old buildings or caves, and they have a few more weeks to go before they hang up in a secure place for their hibernation. As I leave the lochside and walk to my car, a smaller pipistrelle bat follows me along the woodland path. These two species can be confused, but the Daubenton's bat is found over water, while the pipistrelle can be found just about anywhere. There are still plenty of moths out tonight and the bats are doing well. Just before departing, I play a trick on the pipistrelle: I toss a tiny piece of moss above my head and the bat's echo-sounder catches it. The tiny creature swoops down very close to me, but he's not fooled and turns away to hunt a real meal.

The harrier's visit

It is a greyish day today. There is a dampness in the air and not a lot is happening as I walk towards the loch and look across the water towards the island. The tufted duck family and the mallards are happily going about their normal daily routine of feeding in the shallows or preening and resting on the island. A small party of pied wagtails runs around chasing flies on some exposed mud at the edge of the island, while the swan family is down at the far end of the loch scrounging bread from local villagers.

Suddenly there is panic, real panic! Everything is splashing and diving for cover and there is a lot of scolding from the small birds in the bushes. A menacing brown shape comes gliding across the island. It is a hen harrier, in fact a young hen harrier. We call these birds ring tails on account of their brown and black barred tails, because it is very difficult to tell the difference between a young male and a young female. The distinctive white rump flashes as the bird flies across the loch. But when I look at it through my binoculars I see bright flashes of colour on its wings. There is a green flash on its left wing and a pink one on the right. This bird has been wing-tagged, or colour-marked, by an ornithologist studying hen harriers. I know it is a young bird and the colour combination on the wings, I am pretty sure, will tell me that this is a bird which was reared this year at a nest on the moorlands of Easter Ross about 20 miles to the west of the loch. Maybe it is one of the young reared at the nest overlooked by the Forestry Commission's public hide, where visitors can observe the family life of hen harriers in the wild.

These birds breed mainly on the heather moorlands, but in the autumn they disperse quite widely, some of them even reaching the south of England. The colour-marking programme, run by the RSPB, has yielded some very interesting results, showing that some birds move long distances from the north of Scotland to England, while other harriers reared in southern Scotland travel north to spend their winter in the flat coastal lands around the Moray Firth.

The harrier visiting today has had no luck catching small birds around the loch and it flips over the top of the bushes at the far end of the loch and rather aimlessly drifts away, perhaps to hunt in the turnip fields nearby. I wonder where this young bird will journey on to — he will, unfortunately, not always find a welcome.

Glorious autumn

A few weeks ago the hills were at their most lovely, a bright, gaudy purple, the heather in brilliant full bloom. But now, almost all of a sudden, the purple blossom has gone and the hills are starting to look worn; there is a brownish tinge creeping into the scene and it is clear that autumn is approaching fast. Even on the low ground, the trees are looking old and tired, their leaves slowly losing vigour and colour. Although the pace of autumn is unrelenting, it is not a headlong rush towards destruction. The withering process will be slow and dignified and we will have many sunny days of windless calm and balmy interludes. Nevertheless, everywhere wild creatures know that summer is past and autumn is upon us. Unlike us, they must prepare carefully for the future; we just take it as it comes.

Some of the evenings at this time of the year are breathtakingly beautiful. I think there is nothing more pleasurable than to walk

The heather is in bloom and
Scotland's hills (left) are
at their most lovely. A
young hen harrier (above)
flies over the loch scattering
all the small birds in panic.

along the edge of a loch in the Scottish Highlands just before sunset on a late September's day. The water is absolutely motionless, the outlines of the far hills are clear and sharp, there are trails of dusky markings in the sky as the sun sinks over the warm brown distant hills. The golden cast is reflected in the loch, creating beautiful mirror images. Now the nights can be tinged with a hint of frost but the morning chill is soon burnt off by the rising sun.

It has been raining for several days now, and it can surely rain in the Highlands in the autumn. For one or two days it was windy as well, bringing boiling black storm clouds from the Atlantic Ocean to rush eastwards across the Highlands. Today, however, a gentle rain splashes intently on the surface of the loch, the woods are damp and sodden and a smell of moist earth pervades the lochside. But everywhere there is a riot of new colours. Fungi of all sizes, shapes and colours have suddenly appeared around the loch and in the woodland. There are red ones with white spots, small yellow ones, sticky brown ones, tall graceful inkcaps, round puffballs and large mushroom-shaped boletus. The names are also lovely: blushers and blewits, inkcaps and deathcaps, lawyers' wigs and stinkhorns, and very many more with Latin names. Some years are better than others for fungi and the relative preponderance of different species also fluctuates from year to year. Where has this fairytale landscape erupted from, if not by the magic wand of the raingods? Of course, the real body, or mycelium, of the fungi has been growing away all year in the soil or in rotted branches of fallen trees and many other places; but now the fruiting bodies appear as familiar toadstools and mushrooms, throwing out millions of spores to ensure future generations of fungal beauty.

Our cows love boletus mushrooms and when they leave the croft to feed on the common grazing they race each other through the woods searching for the next big juicy boletus. They are like children on a treasure hunt for chocolate as they chase ahead of each other and greedily down another delicious morsel. The boletus is obviously very palatable, considering this gluttonous gallop, but I wonder whether these mushrooms are very nutritious. If nothing else, however, they are obviously a very welcome change of menu for the cattle.

AUTUMN

Many other creatures eat the mushrooms as well. Just here, there's a bit chewed out of that one by a small mouse or vole and here are some black slugs grazing on a white-spotted red-topped fly agaric. Over there something has been nibbling a posy of fallen-over yellow toadstools amongst the most brilliant green moss. Nowadays, with a more wholesome image being promoted for food, many more people are gathering wild mushrooms. Earlier in the day I met a couple walking through the birchwoods searching for yellow chanterelles, one of the most sought-after of all the local fungi. Many local people gather them for money as various firms now buy mushrooms and send them away to markets in the south and on the Continent. There is a whole range of edible mushrooms that more adventurous people have found to their liking, but of course there are others that are poisonous. Even so, we are nowhere near as knowledgeable or dedicated to fungi as other Europeans. The Russians, especially, are avid mushroom hunters and collect many species to eat and to dry for winter use.

Walking on the lochside path, going round past the bay, where the bulrushes grow, a small movement almost under my feet caught my eye. I looked down to find a rather torpid palmate newt dragging itself wearily through the wet leaves. It is time for hibernation and many creatures, including the newts, are preparing for their long winter sleep by returning to their traditional hibernating places. The frogs and toads will also be making ready for their hibernation, and on sunny days I no longer expect to see the lizards basking on warm flat stones.

A lazy trout broke the surface of the loch in the far bay and I idly wondered where these trout try to spawn. This small loch is landlocked and the trout were placed here by the fishing-club members. On many other lochs, at this time of the year, the trout are entering the rivers and burns to search out their ancestral spawning grounds. Here in the clean gravels of the flowing water, the female digs herself a hollow, or redd, in the riverbed to lay her eggs; her mate stays close at her side ready to fertilize the falling eggs. Then they return to the loch and sink down into deeper water for the winter. After hatching, the young trout stay in the flowing water for some years before they

too return to the loch. Salmon are also spawning just now: it is a wonderful sight to come across a pair of spawning salmon in the tiny headwaters of a great river. Their backs are nearly out of the water as they splash and jostle and tussle away in the gravel beds to complete the spawning ritual.

I saw a willow warbler in the lochside alder bushes – one of the last of the autumn, as most of his clan will already be in southern Europe, or even in their winter quarters in Africa. This one was searching amongst the leaves for the last few aphids of the summer, feeding up ready for his journey south. These long-distance migrant birds are ravenous feeders before migration. In general, the warblers need to be leaving in August or early September, when food is still plentiful and they can take advantage of the abundant supply of insects and fruit. They build up fat on the sides of their tiny bodies, which they will use as fuel on their long journey south. This little warbler will increase its weight by nearly a third before it is ready to leave and then one evening it will be up and away. It will fly into the

OPPOSITE AND ABOVE
*Fungi of all sizes, shapes and colours have suddenly
appeared around the loch and in the woodland.*

*Opposite, left: Fly agaric.
Opposite, right: Porcelain fungus.
Above: Orange stag's horn fungus.*

evening sky on the start of its journey, using the stars and the moon
for guidance.

This is a beautiful autumn for rowan berries. Looking across the
water to the far bank, the rowan trees above the loch are laden with
fruit: bunches and bunches of flame-red berries. It is not every year
the rowan trees are so heavily loaded, but, like so many other trees,
every now and then they have a fantastic seed crop and produce
a superabundance of berries to ensure that the thrushes survive and

for our delight, and (the real reason) for the propagation of new rowan trees.

The other day I was looking at the laden rowan in my garden and wondering how much food there really was for wildlife from the rowan harvest. I gathered a bunch and weighed it on the kitchen scales and by estimating how much was left on the tree I calculated that there was nearly a hundredweight and a half of berries on that one tree. When I made a rough calculation of the number of rowan trees in our locality, it was clear that there were many tons of berries – a veritable feast for a whole variety of birds and mammals. Soon, fox and pine marten droppings will be peppered red with the remains of berries.

The fruit is not yet ripe, but nevertheless a pair of mistle thrushes is busy amongst the trees. They are not eating the berries, but just making certain that no one else does! A few moments ago, a female blackbird flew up into the tree and one of the mistle thrushes flew directly at her and bundled her away. They try hard to protect the crop, presumably for the time when they need it most, later in the winter, but they are never really successful up here, because in a few weeks' time thousands and thousands of migrant thrushes, especially redwings and fieldfares, will come down from Scandinavia to devour every berry that is left in Scotland. Now, however, there is still time for the vigilant mistle thrush to think, 'This is my tree and no one else is going to eat my berries.'

Lots of other fruits and seeds are also ripening in the woods. There is quite a substantial crop of nuts on the hazel trees. They are not quite ready, as I find out when I break one open with my teeth: the kernel is about three-quarters formed and still milky-white and soft. In a few weeks they will start to drop to the ground and the voles and mice in the forest will be busy harvesting the fallen crop. They will gather nuts, in between feeding, and transport them down woodland pathways to stores hidden in their warehouse burrows. Already they will have cleaned out their tunnels and refurbished their sleeping quarters. Their new nests will be dry and cosy, a warm bundle of shredded grasses, moss and bark. Soon winter can come and they will be ready.

Autumn gold

Now it is mid-October and the trees are really changing their colours. This is a spectacular time to be in the Scottish Highlands: aspens, birches, willows and rowans are all turning the most beautiful yellows and oranges. I can see a small stand of aspen trees at the far side of the loch on the edge of the slopes leading up to the hill crofts. The leaves are absolutely yellow, as bright as lamplight on the dark hillsides. They tremble in a breeze so light that it hardly stirs the surface of the loch this evening. In the Highlands, local people say that the aspen trembles because the cross of Christ was made out of aspen wood, and the tree must always shudder at the memory of the cruel purpose it served. The birches are a much more vibrant colour, although even amongst them the variety of hues ranges from a thin, pale yellow through orange to flame red. The willows are less boisterous in colour and look a washed-out green.

The roaring of the stags

This evening after dark, as I walked back along the track from my favourite vantage point overlooking the loch nearest to my home, I could hear a stag roaring in the gloomy mountain corries miles away to the south. There's a touch of frost in the air; it is definitely autumn now, with the nights actually longer than the days. Much of the activity in the red-deer herd takes place at night and I can hear one stag challenging another across the corrie. There is a roar and, as if in reply, another roar challenging. I cannot see a thing, but I can imagine the scene: a stag in a hollow on the heather hillside, and with him his group of hinds and their calves from last year; on the slope facing another stag disputing his claim on the hinds and ready to contest the issue.

This is the first autumn I have heard the stags roaring in these particular corries; they are surprisingly close to the township of crofts, but I suppose it's to be expected, as the Scottish red-deer herd continues to grow and grow. Nowadays, it is believed that more than

300 000 red deer live in Scotland and there is considerable concern in most areas that too few are being killed each year by hunters and, consequently, the natural habitat is suffering. The deer eat young trees and shrubs as they start to grow and before they have a chance to reach a safe height. In places, even the remnants of the ancient wood of Caledon, that superb forest of Scots pines, aspens, birches, rowans and junipers, is under threat from too many deer. Their natural predators in Scotland, the wolf and lynx, long ago disappeared

The rowan trees are festooned with sprays of bright red berries.
Right: Fallen branches, autumn leaves and reflections in the loch.

down the path of history, so it is now man's task to make certain that the deer exist in harmony with their environment. At present, we are failing.

The stars are really bright tonight. I can see the Plough and the North Star, and also the moon rising over the hills, casting a silver shadow across the loch. Above the roar of the stag, I can hear a very far-distant clamour from a gaggle of greylag geese, calling as they head over the mountains. Stags roaring and geese calling are two of

the most stirring sounds of autumn in the Scottish hills. Many of the greylag travel south during daylight hours, but some fly over the mountains at night. It is probably safer at night, because some of these small groups of geese, especially when they straggle over the hills or through the mountain passes in bad weather, are liable to be attacked by eagles during the day. The victim is most likely to be a young bird that loses its way or panics at the last moment and breaks away from the skein; when that happens there is a clear possibility that it will be struck down by an eagle. But tonight they will be safe as they call on their way southwards through the hills towards the farmlands of Perthshire. Long ago their way ahead would have been lit only by the celestial bodies, but now the great orange glow from cities like Inverness, Aberdeen, Dundee and Edinburgh will etch the darkened outline of Scotland with motorways of light. I wonder what the young geese think when they see these brilliant illuminations for the first time.

We have now reached the end of October and the tops of the hills are dusted in snow. It really looks like winter and the days are as likely to be windy, wet and snowy, as bright, sunny and frosty. The weather in the Scottish Highlands is never boring, just unpredictable and unreliable. The colour in the birches is now definitely wearing thin. There is just an orange cast in a few trees and the rest are leafless, the sap slowly retreating from the damson-coloured branches. A few alder trees are still showing green, but on the days following a hard night frost, you can see the leaves dropping out of the trees and into the water. The alder does not change colour and the leaves drop off green. This is very valuable where the trees overhang rivers and burns, because the green leaves provide the best of food for invertebrates in the water below and are thus an important part of the food chain for fish.

Despite the approach of winter, there are still some oats left to cut in the fields on the crofts. Long ago, every croft in this area would have grown its patch of oats, maybe 1 acre, or 2 or 3. It was a very important cereal crop. It was food for the crofter as well as his stock, while the straw provided bedding and winter feed for his cattle. A few people still grow oats in the hills and I can see the men working today with a battered old red combine harvester on the hill croft away above the loch. They have just a few acres and it will not take them long to cut the field. This is just as well, as the weather is turning again; it has been so bad that they have not been able to get their harvest in at the usual time and it is nearly the end of October. But I have known times when people have not managed to secure their harvest until well into December and the crop has been under snow at least once.

Twenty years ago this field would have been cut by a reaping machine and then stooked; later the stooks would have been gathered up and built into stacks ready for thrashing later in the winter. A hundred years ago, nearly everyone grew oats, most of which was cut by hand with a sickle or scythe before being tied into sheaves prior to stooking. Hereabouts it was considered lucky to hang a sheaf of corn, from the first swathe cut, in the byre.

Lots of wild creatures eat oats and I wonder as I watch them cut the field today if they might find evidence of badgers, because occasionally some badgers like oats. I remember once they ate the oats in our own fields. We could not understand what had caused the flattened patches in the crop, but once we had cut the field with the combine we could see that the badgers had been coming through the back fence, rolling in the crop and then eating the grain during their night-time visits. They had not eaten all that much and it did not worry us, but we certainly had not realized that they had been feeding on our oats before we started to harvest.

I saw a badger's track when I walked the lochside path the other day. There in the soft earth on the edge of the path was the broad pad of a badger with five toes pointing forwards, quite unlike the four-toed print of a dog or a fox. This is good country for badgers, with the ancient glacial ridges of sand and gravel being ideal for their setts. They prefer to burrow out their huge interconnected homes in dry sandy ground, preferably on a slope, and the local sett is in such a place amongst the birch trees.

At last the drake mallards look like mallards again. For most of the summer they have looked like their mates, speckled brown and rather drab. They acquired their eclipse, or summer, moult plumage after the nesting season, when for a period of a month they were also flightless as they grew new wing feathers. Then they tended to skulk about in the long vegetation around the island, almost ashamed to be seen in their midsummer plumage and only occasionally swimming out to join up with the females and their young on the water. More often than not, they just sulked in cover, sitting around morosely while they moulted into their new winter plumage. Now that they

are back in their resplendent colours, their green heads are bright and iridescent, and they are absolutely spick and span. The grey and brown body, the white collar, the beautiful pale yellow bill and the brilliant little black twisted tail have restored their buoyancy and they are back in circulation again.

At the moment they are bobbing across the loch towards me, thinking I am going to give them some food. Several times a day,

The tracks of badgers are sometimes seen on the lochside path and not far away in the woods is a sett. This badger is eating toadstools.

local people come up to the far end of the loch and throw bread and scraps for the swans and ducks. These ducks have a very easy life: the owner of the loch does not allow any shooting and there is always someone coming up with goodies for them. Mostly it is white bread, but they don't seem to mind if it's white or brown, cut or uncut, wholemeal or plain! I don't know whether they are fat ducks or lazy ducks, but they are certainly well-fed ducks.

Yet at dusk they still appear hungry and set off gently quacking for the stubble fields on the surrounding farms. This is their favourite feeding place at this time of the year. I bet they could hear the noise of the combine harvester today and I wonder if they know which field was being harvested. Will they find the fresh supply of spilt golden grain? They prefer the brightest moonlit nights and then they fly across the whole countryside searching for places to feed. At this time of the year, the ducks really do well with the feeding so easy and convenient. But then they know that within a few weeks life could become very difficult as the ice imprisons the lochs and snow covers the countryside from the high bare peaks to the low-lying farmland beside the sea.

Fogs, frosts and fieldfares

Today I woke up to fog, a cold fog, a frosty fog, one of those first frosty foggy mornings of autumn, or is it winter? It is also uncertain sometimes whether the fog will clear or whether it will be with us all day, clinging to the tips of gloomy pines and depressing further the withering bulrushes. But today it did clear. First the birches and alders threw off their grey mantle and then the hillside appeared, and with a blink of blue sky the countryside slowly struggled free of its gauzy blanket. What a sight was revealed. Everything was overlaid with a beautiful covering of hoar frost.

It's the birch trees that I love most. They are just superb. Every twig, every twiglet is coated with little fingers of frost and they glimmer white in the new morning sun. They stand out brilliantly against the pale-blue sky. Here a group of birches droops over the water, shafts of sunlight filtering through this filigree of iced foliage like sparkling chandeliers. Here a wild dog rose is covered in hoar frost, but the blood-red berries, bright and waxy, are not iced. Only the twigs and thorns have been captured in frost, the defiant flame hips standing out in stark contrast.

And then there are the grasses. The long, yellow, dead grass stems are all gripped by frost. I sit down and look at them: this stem is just superb, the ice in spikelets, like iced hairs covering the blades and stem of the grass, and the weight of the ice causes it to droop its head downwards. Before me is this beautiful, sparkling-white iced meadow and yet I know that in half an hour it will all imperceptibly disappear as the sun burns up into the sky.

Today is 1 November and the Scandinavian thrushes have arrived. I could hear the 'tseep tseep' calls of the redwings and the chuckles of the fieldfares as I went outside just after dawn. Then I saw there were flocks and flocks and more flocks; last night there must have been a tremendous migration over the North Sea from Norway and Sweden. There are thousands of redwings and fieldfares feeding in the rowan trees. They fly around in great chuckling crowds and the skies are alive with flocks of migrating birds. This is autumn migration at its peak. They descend on a rowan tree and voraciously peck at the berries. The trees at the end of the loch have almost lost all their berries already, but up along the fields around the crofts there are trees still heavy with berries and the thrushes are now concentrating their activities in that area.

In the mile or so that I have walked, I have probably seen 5000 or more fieldfares and nearly as many redwings. They have obviously already had a good feed, because when I walked around the far end of the wood there were several hundred redwings perched in the bird-cherry trees, warbling away with their muted sub-song — not the real song of summer, but just a happy chattering call of autumn. These birds will not stay long; they will rest, feed and stay for several days or weeks, but once the berries have gone the majority will head off south into southern Scotland or Ireland or on into England and maybe by the end of the winter they will be away down in Europe. Today, however, those journeys are far in the future and their sole aim is to try to eat every rowan berry in Ross-shire.

OPPOSITE ABOVE
Winter approaches — the days and nights
are getting colder. Hoar frost is
glistening on the long grass in the early-
morning sun.

ABOVE
The redwings are hungrily feasting on
berries after their long flight from
Scandinavia.

LEFT
Every day the greylag geese fly from
their overnight roosts to search for grain
in the stubble fields near the loch.

Gaggles of geese

Today I decided to go goose-watching. I left the small loch and drove across to one of the larger lochs in our area. It is a favourite place for wildfowl in the autumn. Today I reckon there are about 1200 geese on the barley stubbles near the loch; in fact they are all greylags, as this is one of the favourite greylag-geese haunts in Scotland. During the day they search the stubble fields for fallen barley and wheat left over from the harvest and there are thousands in some fields.

When you first look at a big flock of geese it seems like pandemonium, but if you look carefully you see that they are not just a great mass of birds, but that the flocks are made up of lots and lots of families. One family is feeding to the right and meets another family coming the other way; the first has three young while the other has four young. Then you see that several families are moving together − they are probably a related group or small clan. Every now and then a little fight breaks out and the adults sort out the problems. All the time they are searching for and picking up grain; it gives me a chance to look at their lovely grey and brown mottled plumage with white under the tail and the bills and legs orange and pink. Later in the day they will start moving back to the loch to roost and I intend to be there at dusk to watch them flight in.

If you search through the goose flock very carefully, you might find the occasional pink-footed goose, barnacle goose or Greenland white-fronted goose and on a few rare occasions we have seen snow geese in these flocks as well.

I remember once I was at this loch in a particularly good autumn for the geese, which means that it was not a good autumn for the farmers gathering in the harvest. On one farm, the land had become waterlogged and it was impossible for the farmer to harvest one large field of barley; in the end all of it was lost and the geese had a bonanza of feeding for nearly a month. We knew that there were lots of geese that year and we decided to carry out a co-ordinated count at dusk. Flock after flock came pouring into the roost, spiralling down from a height or sometimes hedge-hopping in low over the shore to land in a cacophony of gaggling on the water. When we tallied the counts at the end of the evening, the total was a record-breaking 34 000 greylags coming in to roost on the loch.

Now the light is starting to fade and the geese have been coming in for the last hour. Another flock is falling through the skies. They are so exuberant at this time of year. Some flocks, which have fed further away from the loch, will fly in at maybe 1000 feet or more, calling to the geese already on the loch. Suddenly they come plunging out of the sky, whiffling through space with wings swept back in a mad headlong dive, braking at the very last moment to splash down noisily on to the water. Once on the loch there is a great deal of greeting and ceremony as the numbers continue to swell. It's as though they have so many stories to tell of the day's happenings away from the roost and they all want to cackle them at the same time.

All of these birds are from Iceland, where they nest on lakes and rivers and marshes around the whole country. They usually arrive in October and they will stay with us until next April, when the return flight north takes place. With them today are whooper swans. Some have their long necks and heads stained orangey-brown from feeding in lochs and mires with a high iron content. When adult, they are pure white, with bright yellow and black bills. The young birds of the year are buffy white all over and their bills are pale pink and black. The number of whooper swans coming to this loch in the autumn can vary from year to year. Today there are about 200 with the geese; in some years there are very many more. They have also been feeding on the stubble fields during the day and have come back to roost on the loch for the night.

OVERLEAF
Whooper swans arrive from Iceland
in October to spend their winter
feeding on farmland and roosting
on the lochs.

This is a large loch, relatively shallow, with not much water flowing in or out through the small burns. In fact it lies in a basin surrounded by fertile farmland and over the years the make-up of the loch has changed. It has been affected by the run-off from agricultural land and an increasing influx of nutrients has changed its biological composition. Every four or five years pondweeds explode in a riot of lush growth and the loch is absolutely clogged with plants. In those autumns the wild swans love this place and gorge themselves on the succulent weed.

One November we found nearly 2000 swans resident on the loch. It was the most spectacular sight as you looked across from the road. Flock after flock of swans was dotted across the surface of the water. They were feeding in family parties, just like the geese on the stubbles, and were busy upending and pulling up weed from the bed of the loch. As you looked, half the birds had their tails out of the water and the other half were busily chewing up the weed that they had pulled up.

When you looked more closely, you saw that each swan had an attendant audience: a small party of wigeon and a few coot waiting for scraps of vegetation. The smaller ducks cannot get at the food as easily as the swans with their long necks, so, as the swans fed by pulling up weed, the ducks busily cleaned up the scraps. It really was a spectacle: almost 2000 swans surrounded by about 8000 wigeon. The collective sound of over 10 000 wildfowl feeding in a comparatively small area of water was something that had to be heard to be believed. This autumn the loch is quite different; there is no massive growth of weed and the swan numbers are much lower.

The advance of winter

The trees now are bare of leaves, as I walk round the edge of the loch. A few blue tits are feeding in the alder trees, searching in crevices in the bark for unsuspecting insects or their eggs. It's much colder today and the ice on the loch is just firm enough for the ducks to be standing around near the island. The coots have gone; they must have decided that the ice was going to cover the whole of the loch and that they should take off before the surface was completely frozen over. The tufted ducks have also gone. They have been here all autumn and I was surprised that they had not left earlier, but overnight they had clearly decided that it was time for them too to go to the estuary. The mallards will probably hang on here for a few more days because, at least, they know people will come and feed them on the ice; but I suspect that even they will go down to the shore if the ice continues to thicken on the loch.

The estuary is not very far away — it is only a couple of miles down to the bay, where thousands of waders and wildfowl spend the winter. The mute swan family flew down there over a month ago to join up with other mute swan families from around the firth. The bays around the shore are rich in food, especially at low tide when the mud and sands are full of invertebrates and there is a rich growth of zostera or eel grass.

At high tide the waders and wildfowl gather together on the salt marsh, but when the tide turns, as it does twice in every twenty-four hours, and the water starts to ebb, the mud is exposed and the birds can start to feed again. There are oystercatchers, curlews, redshanks and dunlins, wigeon, teal and mallard as well as black-headed, common and herring gulls. A whole variety of different kinds of birds live in these estuaries during the winter. Only in the very severest frost will the mud flats actually freeze, but at the moment the feeding is plentiful, despite the fact that just a couple miles away the loch is gripped in ice and there is no food there for the ducks.

The days now are very short, but some of the sunsets are beautiful and so are the dawns. Today, just after 7 a.m. I woke to find the sky in the south-east a deep dusky pink which deepened to rose red as the sun pushed up from behind the low hills. In fact the brightest

OVERLEAF
*Ducks roosting on the loch
against the setting sun of
an autumn day.*

colours are often before the sun rises above the horizon. In the evening the colours seem to linger longer and there are often scattered clouds across the sky, black streaks, orange bands, pale green-blue patches of buttermilk sky in a washed-out November day.

The chaffinches are now in flocks, mainly feeding around the farms, and as I drove towards the loch today several hundred flew up in rather a fluster into the trees alongside a farm field. I could see the reason for their panic, as a male sparrowhawk dashed along the hedge with smooth precision, across the path of my car and disappeared into the pine plantation towards the loch. He had failed to kill — maybe it was my car that disturbed him, or at least disturbed the birds he was hunting — but there will be another chase and another attempt to get a meal before night closes in once again.

This evening, as I came away from the loch, I saw the start of an eclipse of the moon. By the time I got home, I was able to watch the full eclipse in the gaps between the scudding clouds. It was very slow; in fact, it did not seem to be happening and then suddenly the moon was missing. Nowadays all is explained to us and we are told what is going to happen by radio and television. How different it was long ago. I wonder what early man thought was happening as the moon disappeared in the night sky.

Yet our ancestors made much more use of the moon and in ancient times the northern people would have been lost without it. The Standing Stones at Callanish, on the Isle of Lewis in the Hebrides, are an outstanding example of how late-Neolithic man used the moon for quite complex geometric and astronomical observations. Stonehenge, by contrast, was used for solar calculations. It staggers me to read of the accuracy with which these ancient people built their stone circles and how exact they were with their measurements. At Callanish, the moon appears to skim the southern horizon for a few days every eighteen and a half years. At these times it rises a few degrees east and sets a few degrees west of south, while slightly further north it doesn't rise at all. The folk at Callanish clearly knew of this lunar cycle and I can imagine they might have been able to predict eclipses. I wonder if they understood them, or if they were terrified of the awesome celestial phenomena like that which occurred tonight.

The last dance

Another day, another mood. In fact, it was a quite lovely day today, as I snatched a quick lunchtime stroll round the lochside path. The grey-green lichens festooning the willows were at their very best against the skeletal bushes and the soft, low sunlight. A green woodpecker yaffled in the distance – not a common sound in these parts, but this species has recently started to colonize the eastern Highlands. The rabbits in the croft fields were chasing each other near the warrens and I suppose that was the only omen of approaching winter. My old neighbour always says, 'It's a bad sign to see rabbits out all day at this time of the year: they are feeding up before bad weather.' We'll see.

WINTER

There was a forecast of heavy snow in the north of Scotland when I arrived at Heathrow airport to join the evening flight to Inverness. The forecast was accurate; the familiar lights of Inverness were barely visible through the blizzard as we descended through snow-laden clouds towards the Moray Firth. My drive home over the mountains was slow, my headlights only just piercing the heavily falling snow. There was no wind and no drifting — thank goodness. The snow was just falling straight out of the sky in large soft flakes and I was glad to get home that night.

It was a real snow storm and in the morning everything was covered in deep snow, the birches overwhelmed by the heavy weight of snow and great branches breaking from the ancient pines. A male pheasant (above) searches for food in the snowy scene.

WINTER

Next morning, 16 December, at dawn the snow was still falling, falling thickly and ceaselessly, with no wind at all and in ominous silence. Everything and everywhere – cars, houses, powerlines, trees – were already covered in over a foot of snow and there were no signs in the grey skies that it was going to stop. The weather reports were of continuing heavy snowfalls all over the north of Scotland, with power blackouts, traffic chaos and many roads already closed. The police warned repeatedly against making non-essential journeys. As morning progressed, the snow on the trees got thicker and thicker and also damper and damper. It was not feather-light snow but heavy, sticky snow. A short walk into the forest near my home was punctuated by the crash and crack of breaking branches, straining under the great weight of snow. This was no time to walk in the wood, as another large branch crashed to the ground, a cloud of blinding snow obscuring the ancient pine just like the aftermath of a giant explosion.

By now there were nearly 2 feet of level, heavy snow and the trees were looking extremely sad; the slender birches were almost bent double as they succumbed to the weight of the snow and many snapped like matchsticks. The great Caledonian pines in the forest were just cascades of snowy branches, some reaching to the ground and others torn asunder where huge limbs had been wrenched out from the trunk to fall on the forest floor. The juniper bushes were buried, hidden under mountains of weighty wet snow.

Apart from the cracking of branches, the countryside was silent, so quiet as it lay immobile under the heavy soundproofing of thick snow. Wildlife was also silent and noticeably absent. What were the squirrels thinking in their dreys as their world crashed about their ears? I suppose, like us, they were waiting for the snowstorm to pass and then they would decide how serious their situation was. This is the time when winter really affects animals that graze on vegetation and search for food on the forest floor. Of course, mice and voles can work away under deep snow and their stores of nuts are always available underground. But many animals, like deer and hares, find it very difficult to get to food in deep snow. It is marvellous, though, how nature works. The heavy snow has smashed down so many branches that there are already fresh supplies of food for animals in the soft green pine tips that have fallen from the very tops of the trees. Soft, succulent bark, which until now has been well away from gnawing teeth.

At the moment no one is moving, not even us. We can get our tractor around to the cattle, but our cars are stranded. We will need to wait until we can snowplough our own way to the county road: there is no way that the big snowploughs will come along our little road when there is such chaos on the major roads and much work to be done to renew communications. For the present, it is time to marvel at nature's work – the fury that caused it and the beauty it created; to enjoy this stunning new landscape. Already by mid-afternoon there is a slight wind stirring from the west and there is a rushy noise in the forest as the pine needles shake themselves. An hour later a fresh wind is blowing – a soft wind, with no real chill in it; in fact, there is no frost in the ground, so this snow, despite its depth, will not last for long.

The lochs are only lightly frozen, so the heavy snow in the water has turned into a soggy brown mass on the edge of the loch, a brown peaty slush slopping around at the bank side. The wind is starting to liven up the water and to shake the trees, discarding snow everywhere. A few branches, which were broken earlier but didn't fall, loosen in the wind and crash to the ground in a dump of snow. This is not a time to walk through the woods to the loch; it is a time to stay clear and wait for a peaceful tomorrow. By evening much of the snow has disappeared from the trees and already there are the first signs of a thaw as the snow begins to shrink.

The cattle are anxiously waiting for their hay today; they have stamped out a flat area in the snow on the edge of the forest fields and when we take the tractor and hay to them they are eager to feed. Breaking open the bales of hay and scattering it on the ground immediately attracts a hungry robin searching for food, and as I leave the herd there are two robins and three yellowhammers feeding right amongst the hooves of the cattle. I expect the yellowhammers are getting seeds from the grass bales and the robins will be searching for the odd insect that has been baled with the dry grass at hay time.

Next day, most of the snow has gone. This time it came quickly and it went quickly and we are back to a relatively mild winter's day, but there are floods in the valley following such a rapid thaw. The wise farmers will have already moved their stock before the river swells with the snow melt.

Cold days and colder nights

Today is the winter solstice: the day with the fewest hours of sunlight in the year. Here in the north of Scotland it is light just after 8 a.m. and the sun climbs slowly into the sky and hardly clears the higher hills to the south. By 4 p.m. it has already dipped into dusk. It is a very short day for wildlife. For us it is easy, as we can go into the house, turn on the lights and heat, and forget about the long winter's night, but for small birds in particular these are long and difficult nights to survive.

As I walked along the lochside today, I looked across at the bulrushes, standing very silent, touched by a slight frostiness and a skin of ice on the water below. A small band of long-tailed tits came bobbing along through the lichen-shrouded willow bushes, landed briefly on the heads of the bulrushes and picked around searching for insects. It really must be hard work finding hibernating insects, tucked away in crannies in the bark of trees, or in the lichens and leaves and the stems of bulrushes. Maybe there are a few seeds as well. They look so fragile – pinky-white and black balls of fluff, tiny black and white striped heads, long black tail and just under 10 grams in weight.

I often get cold, even with my down jacket, thick trousers, woolly hat and gloves, yet these little birds have to keep warm throughout the long winter nights. It is important for them to find not only

OPPOSITE
A red deer stag in winter;
Scotland's deer population is at
a record high.

enough food during the day but also a good place to roost at night. All the small birds have the same problem: the blue tits, great tits and coal tits which feed around the loch, as well as the wrens scolding from the sedges on the island. This evening, and every evening, they will need to find somewhere dry and warm to spend the night. It is just before 4 p.m. and the long-tailed tits head off, clearly knowing where they are going tonight. In their home range there will be several places where they know they can find a dry and cosy spot to pass the night: maybe a hole in a tree, or a broken branch, where they can snuggle together to keep warm. It is most important to be dry and in the coldest periods of winter it makes sense to roost closely together. At other times, when it is not raining and snowing, they will roost side by side on a branch tightly packed together tail to head to tail.

The tiny treecreepers also have an interesting way of keeping warm during winter. There are a couple of giant redwood trees, from North America, growing beside a big house about half a mile from the loch which were planted in the last century. The bark of the redwood is very soft and the treecreepers excavate a round hole, the size of a small apple, in the soft fibrous orange bark. If you look at these trees carefully you will usually find three or four or five of these special roosting holes around each trunk. Depending upon which way the wind is blowing, the treecreeper will choose comfortable roosting sites away from cold and wet winds. I remember one night going with a torch and looking at the redwood trees near my home and there were two treecreepers in different holes in the redwood bark. They were just cuddled-up, fluffy balls: it was difficult to see that they were birds rather than a bundle of feathers.

Wrens are also very skilled at keeping warm and in the coldest periods of winter, instead of roosting singly or in twos or threes, wrens will come from a considerable distance to join together in a communal roost. There have been sightings of twenty or even thirty wrens entering a hole under the eaves of a house or in an old shed or a hollow tree. In these roosts, a whole bundle of wrens will be sleeping together during the night to gain maximum body heat and thus to survive and hunt for another day.

Treading the ice

The surface of the loch is still, absolutely mirror-like, and in the late evening the reddening skies are perfectly reflected in the water. It is one of those most beautiful, calm, clear days of early winter. High above me, boisterous flights of rooks and jackdaws are going to roost, tumbling untidily through the skies, hundreds of excited, squawking birds. The normal winter roost flights are heads-down, no-nonsense journeys through wet and windy evenings straight to the roost wood. Today there is time for rooks and jackdaws to gambol and play, to circle and to gain height, to rise several thousand feet into the sky and to swirl in noisy gambolling flocks. All day they have been scavenging for food on the farm fields throughout the surrounding countryside; now they are homing in from several different directions and heading for the big roost wood down near the shore. There, some 10 000 or more rooks and jackdaws will spend the night in a cosy wood of thick Scots pine.

It's fun watching them fly over the loch, especially as the sun sinks over the hill and the beautiful oranges and reds of a winter sunset illuminate the bare trees at the far side of the loch. At this time of the year the trees are like skeletons in the evening light, the straight stems of birches, the spreading branches of alder trees, the thick bushy outlines of the old Scots pines and, in the back behind them, far, far away, thin black clouds streak the sky. Then it is dark, really dark, and the first tawny owl hoots from the hollows behind the loch. This is the time of year when still evenings resound to the calls of tawny owls — they are persuading their youngsters to leave

OVERLEAF
Flocks of jackdaws join with rooks at dusk in the big roost wood near the loch. On fine evenings flocks of hundreds gambol through the sky but in bad weather they fly low and fast to their night-time shelter.

home. A few young owls of the year are still in the territories belonging to the adults and their parents are already thinking ahead towards spring, so there is much 'hooting' and 'kewicking' – a really ghostly racket goes on as they try to sort out ownerships and hoot farewell to their large young.

We have now had several days of really cold weather. The temperature dropped down to $-10°$, $-12°$, $-14°C$ and the ice grew thickly on the lochs for several days. There was no snow, the countryside was dry and cold, the ground rang like iron and we were in the real grip of winter. One day I had a chance to test the ice. I walked gently out on to the loch and there was not a sign of it breaking. I jumped up and down. There was that hard ringing sound, the ice being clear and green – in fact, so clear that you could see through to the vegetation on the bed of the loch: that is really hard ice. I kicked a stone out from the bank and sent it curling across the surface of the frozen loch. I was even able to walk to the island, my dogs gambolling along beside me, and after carefully testing the ice I realized that I could walk right across the loch. I could explore the island, which is usually a boggy, oozing marsh, impossible to walk across. There would be other people watching the ice carefully and, if the frost continued until the weekend, I felt sure this would be the opportunity for a bonspiel – an outdoor curling match.

By the weekend the largest loch in the area was also frozen solid. The telephones had been working overtime and on Saturday morning the lochside road was thronged with cars. Folk from far and near were putting on extra-warm clothes and unloading their curling stones. The winters are no longer as cold as they were earlier this century, so nowadays most curlers play only on artificial ice rinks indoors. But the chance of a real outside match is too much to miss. The sport went on until dusk, a happy chattering band matching their skill with the curling stones on natural ice and swapping stories with many a dram of pure malt whisky.

Trials of life

Today I saw the glint of a metal ring on a bird's leg. It was a blue tit, feeding among the willows at the western edge of the loch. There was a small group of blue tits and great tits searching busily for insects and one of them, this young blue tit, had a bright shiny ring on its leg. I could tell it was a young bird, because its plumage was rather greeny-blue instead of the bright blue of an adult bird. This bird is already a winner in blue-tit society.

What do I mean by saying it's a winner? It was ringed by one of my friends in a woodland not far away, where he has put up a lot of nest boxes. He is a keen bird-ringer and he goes round his nest boxes in May and June to ring all the young birds. This bird was probably one of those broods. He has ringed there for many years, so we can use for our comparison a brood of blue tits he ringed five years ago. It is very difficult to follow them, as very few are ever found dead and just as few are recaught when he goes around the nest boxes in the spring. These chance happenings tell us something about the lives of the birds, but we have to imagine most of it.

Let's take an average family where there are nine chicks in the nest when he rings them. A few days later they are ready to leave, but one does not make it — the runt of the family. It is left to die in the box when the others leave, as it is just not strong enough to fly up to the hole and out with its eight brothers and sisters. For the first few days they stay close to the tree in which their nest box was fixed. Here, amongst the oaks, the birches and the willows, they perch and chatter and wait for their parents to come back with caterpillars. Quite often they perch in a little band, all close together on a small branch, waiting for their parents to return. There is sometimes a lot of squabbling over who is going to sit in the middle and keep warm and who is going to sit at the chilly end of the branch. One day there is an argument, a lot of chittering and pushing, and suddenly one poor youngster falls to the ground. That was a mistake and you must not make mistakes in nature. The noise attracts a tiny weasel and when the fluttering bundle hits the ground, as quick as a flash, the weasel is on it and chick number eight makes a meal.

WINTER

LEFT
For small birds, very cold weather is a hazardous time.
Fighting in the snow is not a wise activity and these blue tits
should be feeding and keeping dry and warm.

RIGHT
Our loch is starting to freeze over as the temperature falls;
soon all the ducks will depart for the estuary and the ice
may be thick enough for us to walk on the frozen loch.

WINTER

As they grow older and bolder, the blue tits move further afield. One day, as they fly from one group of willows to the next, a deadly grey shape streaks across the meadow and, wham, the blue-tit chick ends up in the talons of a sparrowhawk, a meal for his young in the pine thicket west of the loch. During the autumn, two more are lost, one in a smash-and-grab raid by a feral cat and the other knocked down by a speeding car. Young blue tits have so little time to learn that fast-moving objects are dangerous.

As autumn approaches, they disperse more widely. They have a very easy time in the reed beds and all of them survive that period. Then they move to the houses on the edge of the wood. Here they find easy feeding at the nut bags, but one young blue tit makes a mistake, flies through the window thinking that it is an opening to the other side, and, with a bang, breaks his neck. Another one dies during the winter: he gets wet, roosts in the wrong place and, during the long, cold, wet night, he gets colder and colder and in the morning he is dead.

The following spring, two birds remain and they both nest, one in a hole in an oak tree and the other in a nest box. One is a female and she successfully rears five young; the other is a male and they lose their eggs to squirrels. The following winter, the female is dead: she is caught by a sparrowhawk dashing with deadly precision through the wood. The one remaining blue tit returns to its nest box the next spring and is caught by the bird ringer. It survives and for the next three summers he retraps this particular bird, by which time it is a very old blue tit indeed — one of the truly amazing survivors. So I'm afraid the blue tit I saw today with a ring has a much greater chance of dying than it does of surviving to breed next spring.

New Year turbulence

If December was cold, then New Year brought dramatic change — it is now 14°C above freezing! The warmth on New Year's Day was amazing. How unpredictable is Scotland's weather. In other parts of the northern world you know that when it snows and the frosts come in October it is not going to change until the following April or May. Throughout the winter days of northern Russia or North America it will remain cold right through the winter. I remember once staying in a ranger's station high in the Bitterroot mountains of Montana at the end of October, when overnight snow totally transformed the wilderness. My hosts immediately organized my retreat to the valley, saying that this mountain pass would now remain unopened until the following May. But here in Scotland we can have weeks of freezing cold winds, frozen lochs and snow-covered hills, and then suddenly the soft westerly wind blows from the Atlantic Ocean and it all changes. The snows melt, the lochs thaw, the ground is again soft and even the grass starts to grow in the middle of winter. That is how it is today.

The rivers are swollen with floods from heavy rain and melting snow and the low-ground farmers, worried about their stock, move sheep and cattle from the riverside meadows on to higher ground, while roads and fences have disappeared under water. There is a very high wind today, raging through forests and galloping over hills. All night it pounded our house and roared down the chimneys with some gusts of well over 100 miles per hour. The surface of the loch is churning — no real waves, just heavy trembling. But it is relatively calm here compared to the open seas and my mind, as I look across the loch, is not really here but up in Shetland, where the morning news told of disaster. A stricken oil tanker has crashed on to the rocks at the southern end of Shetland. Around our loch the only worry for the birds and animals is where to find food and then a dry bed for the night, but in Shetland the first of the sea birds, otters and seals will have found their homes covered in thick black oil. It's thirty-five years since I first walked on the beautiful white sands of Quendale Bay; tonight the TV programmes will show the sad oily destruction of that pristine beach.

A cormorant is on the loch today, all by himself swimming and diving. He looks entirely at home on his solo ploy. On one dive he came up with a small eel wriggling violently in his bill and it took him a long time to subdue it. Several times he dropped it into the water and then recaptured it. Finally he managed to swallow it. He swallowed it very slowly, head first, and his neck was stretched and wriggling as he tried to down his meal. In fact, even when there was no sign of the eel outside his bill, you could see it struggling inside his throat. Then he stood up and shook his wings, dipped his bill into the water to wash it and slipped under the surface again to search for more food. It is unusual to see a cormorant on this loch and it probably means that there are very few sprats and young herrings in the Beauly Firth this winter. Instead of feeding in a great flock of 500 or 600, each cormorant is having to find fish in lochs, rivers and along

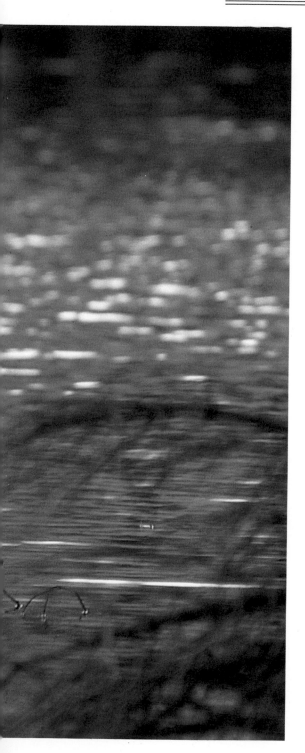

LEFT

A solitary cormorant was fishing the loch and after eating an eel, he roosted on a low branch jutting from the water.

ABOVE

Three waxwings flew across the island as I left. This is a good winter for this beautiful bird from Scandinavia.

the coasts, where hunting is much more difficult than diving into great shoals of winter sprats. His swimming round past the island made me look again at the beautiful grey-green lichens growing all over the willow bushes on the island. Here lichens grow in wild and profuse abandon because the air is pollution free; the twigs and the branches of the trees in this area are just hanging with beards of lichens.

Just before I left the waterside, I saw the cormorant jump out of the water to roost on a low branch jutting from the lochside. Then three waxwings flew across the bushes on the island, moving very fast. They did not stop and it was only their direct flight, rather like a starling's, and their shrill little calls which allowed me to identify them. These are very beautiful winter visitors from Scandinavia and do not come every winter, or rather they do not come in large numbers every winter, but once or twice a decade we get lots and lots of them in the north of Scotland. This winter is one of those special years.

The waxwings start to arrive in early November, and by December and January there are often flocks of up to thirty or forty scattered through the countryside. These little groups of waxwings quickly learn their local patch and early on they know the best places in the forest for rowan berries. They will also have located the wild rose bushes, ready to eat the rich red hips softened by the frost. Juniper bushes, thick in berries, will also be on their map. They travel too to the villages and towns, where they search out cotoneaster bushes covered in orangey-red berries. A week ago a small group of fourteen were in our garden and we were thrilled when they spent the whole morning with us. It was one of those lovely springlike days in mid-January, which we all know is just a passing delight. They ate a few rowan berries from the tree at the back of the house and then, as they perched on the ridge of the house, they saw that the warming winter sun was stirring a few bluebottle flies from under the slates. The flies were still very sleepy and easy to catch and these beautiful birds were flying out to fly-catch just above our heads.

The waxwing is a really beautiful bird, on account of the extraordinarily lovely colours in its wing. If you look very closely, you can see that the innermost wing feathers have brilliant red waxy tips. The feather itself is grey-brown with a white flash near the end, and then comes this brilliant red spiky tip, rather like red sealing wax, while the outer feathers are tipped with brilliant yellow and white flashes at the very ends of the wing.

Suddenly there is a shrill trilling call and they are off, flying fast and direct into the powder-blue winter sky. It looks as though they have had a signal and know exactly where to go. I wonder if they are seeking juniper berries or rose hips, or have they decided to do the 2-mile trip to the local village and gorge on cotoneaster berries? In spring they leave us and head away north to the vast boreal forests of Scandinavia and Russia. And we are the poorer when they go, with their confiding nature, captivating beauty and sweet chatterings on our rose hips.

Otters in the snow

Tonight the still air was pierced by the calling of foxes. They were down in the boggy ground between the loch and the forest. The shrill yapping of the dog fox was answered by the yowl of a vixen. January is the time when foxes come together and February is the commonest month for them to mate. At this time of the year they are at their most vocal – not every night, but suddenly one night you hear the yapping bark of a dog fox across the mosses and then occasionally the squalling cry, the most incredible hullabaloo, uttered by the female. The dog fox can occasionally make this noise, and it sends a shudder through me and also my dogs, who have hysterics if they hear a fox howling down in the forest. The young foxes are born just over fifty days after mating and by that time the female will have chosen the best earth, or breeding hole, for their arrival.

All this is going on in the woods and around the lochs, but mostly we see nothing of it. We see the occasional fox slip through the headlights of the car as we travel the country roads, or we hear their calling on starlit nights, or sometimes we see a red fox slink through the bushes during the day. But when there is snow on the ground, we can really see what has been going on at night all around us. Last evening there was a fall of an inch or so of snow and this morning the countryside is covered in a white mantle. The loch is frozen and there is an inch or two all the way across its surface. As I walk the lochside path, I can see the tracks of different animals and birds.

A pheasant has walked out across the ice, maybe for 100 yards, and then turned round and come back again. Each foot is directly behind the other, but the track is really wiggly, like a drunken man struggling along a street. Just a few feet from the bank, a fox has

BELOW
The stoats are now in their white
ermine coats hunting through the snow
for small rodents and rabbits.

OPPOSITE
Today, the tracks on the snow-covered
loch revealed the true extent of
the night-time activities.

crossed the pheasant's track, very doglike in character: he has gone straight from one bank to the other, cutting off a corner of the loch. He will have been searching for voles along the bankside vegetation and, on this occasion, on the rushy island as well. Further on, there is the small track of a stoat and evidence of a scuffle under the snow where the grass has been torn up. I wonder if he was successful in catching a mouse, or whether it was a missed opportunity. At this time of the year, some of the stoats are pure white. One that I saw a few days ago had a little brown patch on his face; otherwise his beautiful ermine coat was a perfect dazzling white in the snow, with just a black tip to his white tail. There are quite a few signs of rabbits, and also the larger tracks of a brown hare which has crossed the path and gone down on to the meadow by the edge of the farm.

One winter, in just such conditions, I had the most beautiful sight of some otters playing in the snow. Although I did not see them actually in the snow, I saw their heads in the water as they moved off down along the small river. But where the river came out of the loch, the water was frozen and the banks were covered in snow, and you could see the very distinctive tracks of otters, with their tails trailing behind them over the snow. In a few places, where the ground sloped down towards the loch, the otters had been sliding on their bellies. They just love tobogganing down snow banks and, from following the tracks, you could really sense the enjoyment and fun these graceful creatures had gained from playing in the snow. In another place they had bounded over a bank and followed each other down, sliding to the water's edge.

Otters move a lot at this time of the year: they can be on our loch for only a day, catching a few eels amongst the tangled roots of the alder trees; on the other hand, they might make an overnight visit, but we have no way of knowing if they dropped in. They will follow the rivers and burns and even small ditches, calling in at little ponds *en route*. Some of the time they will be down on the seashore among the seaweed-covered rocks, a mile or more away, and at other times they will head up one of the bigger rivers, where they will spend more time searching for fish. I suppose they might travel 4 or 5 miles, or more, during a period of just a couple of weeks and somewhere in this large home range they will decide to have their young in the spring.

There was more snow this evening, but this time it came with a wind, a cruel blustery wind which whipped the snowy spindrift into your eyes and clogged your nostrils as you walked. The dogs just did not like it – this was not 'walkies', this was a hard slog. Normally my dogs enjoy rushing around in the snow like children, but today it was 'keep your nose down time'; as soon as you stop, turn your back into the wind. The cows had their backs to the wind as well, tucked in against the forest shelter. There were a few partridges trying to dig through the snow cover, but this was not the time to find food, it was the time to shelter.

The snow really is a very useful way of knowing what is happening when you are not around to see. One of my friends illustrated this point with a personal experience. He had killed a deer on his farm and the lower part of the legs were left on a table in the shed where he had cleaned the animal. He meant to throw them in a bag or burn them the next day. But they sat on the table for a few more days. One day one of the legs was missing. He could not understand it, because he knew the shed was secure from cats and dogs and he had no rats. Intrigued, he left the three legs on the table and, sure enough, next morning another leg was missing. He was really confused. He searched around in the shed and there was absolutely no sign of it. Two nights later, the next leg disappeared and again he was puzzled, but guessed an animal had taken it – but how, and what animal? The following night it snowed; there were 2 inches of snow in the morning when he woke up. He went out to the shed, sure that he would solve the mystery and certain that another leg would be missing. The last leg had indeed gone. But that morning the evidence was plain to see: a stoat had come in through the small hole under the door, climbed the wooden table, grabbed the last leg, just as it had done the rest, pulled it off the table and dragged it out under the door. Because of the snow, the track of the stoat was easy to follow across the yard and into the shed full of hay. Undoubtedly, when the hay was finished in the spring he would find the remains of the four legs, where the stoat had made a meal off the pickings on the roe deer's legs.

*Red squirrels are busy in the
pine woods feeding on the bumper
crop of cones in the woods
around the loch.*

Ancient wood of Caledon

There are people talking and calling in the woods today, in a place where I normally never expect people to be. The track around the loch is often used by people, who come to enjoy the beauty of the loch and the quietness and the enjoyment of a walk through lovely countryside, or who come to the end of the loch to feed the swans and the ducks in the spring and the summer, until the birds leave in the late autumn. But today the noises of people are in a thicker part of the pine wood. It is January, and this year the Scots pines are laden with cones and the chatter is from the cone-pickers.

In various parts of the Scottish Highlands people still pick cones in January. They gather them from the trees in baskets, reaching high up into the branches and pulling off the developing cones. The cones are taken away in sacks to nurseries, where they are heated gently in a kiln and encouraged to open to allow the pine seeds to fall out. The seeds are gathered and dried and used in nurseries for growing new Scots pine seedlings. Some of the woods are special genetic stock, where the purest Scots pine trees grow, and these are highly prized by foresters for restocking native pine woods.

There are many other creatures who know this is a good year for pine cones. I have seen more red squirrels recently, busy in the trees surrounding the loch, also pulling off the pine cones. But instead of putting them in sacks, they run with a cone to sit on a broad branch and gnaw their way in, pulling off each bract of the cone and extracting the seed lying beneath. Once they have winkled out all the seeds, they drop the remaining cone stem to the ground. This evidence of squirrels is very plentiful at the moment, with chewed-up cones scattered like apple cores under the trees.

In the Highlands we just have red squirrels, although a few grey squirrels are starting to penetrate the mountain barrier, either by the Western route up through Argyllshire, or by the east through Deeside and Aberdeenshire. Let's hope they never take over in this area as elsewhere, because it is so pleasing to see such high numbers of red squirrels. In some places they are so plentiful that they come into people's gardens and feed on the bird tables. I know one lady who has half a dozen squirrels or more as regular visitors to her nut bags and bird tables. At times some become very tame and easy to approach. This year they should have a good breeding season, because food is so plentiful and the animals themselves will be in good condition after a bountiful crop of pine cones.

There is also a bird which is pleased to find a rich cone harvest on the Scots pine this year. This is a very special bird – the Scottish crossbill. A member of the finch family, it is quite a bulky little bird about 5 inches long. The males are red and the females are greeny or yellowish-green. The crossbill, as the name implies, has a very distinctive feature in that the bill is crossed at the tip, the upper mandible crossing over the lower one. This specially shaped bill is for opening pine cones and extracting the seeds. The Scottish crossbill differs from the one which occurs throughout continental Europe by having a larger bill for opening the heavier cones of the Scots pine tree rather than the lighter cones of spruces.

This January there have been a lot of crossbills in the woods. You do not see them very often, but tend to hear them, with their loud 'chup, chup' calls echoing through the tops of the trees. Sometimes you know that they are there only because, as you walk along, a pine cone drops to the floor. You look up and see this parrot-like little bird crawling around in the high foliage of the Scots pine tree. Crossbills deal with cones in a quite different way to the squirrels. The squirrel chews it away until just the stem of the cone is left, but the crossbill opens each individual section of the cone carefully, bends back the bract and extracts the seed with its crossed bill; once the cone is empty of seeds it is dropped to the forest floor.

They build their bulky nests in the very outermost branches of the Scots pines. Yet another unusual feature of this bird is that, in Scotland, they can nest in just about any month of the year. They will even nest in January, when there is snow on the ground and the young crossbills almost 'hibernate' between feeding times. The parents feed them with regurgitated pine seeds, bringing a whole crop full of seeds back to the nest to feed to their young – a sort of milky, soupy mix of half-digested pine seeds.

There is an interesting fable about crossbills. It is believed that the reason they have a red plumage and a crossed bill is because this was the bird that tried to wrench the nails out of the hands of Christ as he was nailed to the cross. Ever since, the bird has had a crossed bill and a red breast.

The horse of the woods

There are a couple of other birds which, from a British point of view, are special to the pine forests of northern Scotland. One is the little crested tit, the size of a blue tit, with its very distinctive plumage. The bird is generally brown, but the head has a beautiful little black and white crest, with a black mark running through the eye and a very distinctive black bib. These birds are found principally in old Scots pine forests in the northern part of Scotland, especially the old Caledonian forests of Strathspey and Glen Affric. Here, in Scotland, crested tits prefer the old forests, which have a thick undercover of heather, blaeberry and juniper bushes as well as dead trees, where in spring they excavate a nest hole in the rotten wood. They have a lovely churring call and sometimes when a band of coal tits moves through the woods by the loch I hear a couple of crested tits churring from the pines.

At the other extreme is a massive bird which you occasionally come across in winter in the pine woods; it is one which you can't miss. Suddenly there is a great blundering crashing sound as the cumbersome bird lifts out of the foliage of a Scots pine and crashes through the wood. This is a capercaillie, the turkey-sized game bird, which in Britain is found only in the pine forests of Scotland. At this time of the year it is mainly feeding on the broad tops of the pines, especially the flat-topped, old Scots pine trees, where it wanders across the top of the tree, grazing on the pine needles, in particular those which have recently grown after previously being grazed by capercaillies. In winter time the birds live principally on pine needles.

The male is a very large bird, nearly as big as a turkey, and is generally black all over. If you get the chance to look at one closely, you will notice that the body is tinged with a green iridescence. The

neck has grey-edged feathers, which form a sort of ruff and a distinctive beard in the older birds. The wings are rich brown, with a distinctive white flash at the shoulder, while the broad tail, which is spread during display, has white flecks and spots on it. The bill is heavy and yellow or ivory coloured and there is a brilliant red wattle above the eye. The female is half the size and a beautiful patterned mix of browns, buffs and greys. She lays her eggs on the forest floor.

In March, the capercaillies start to visit their leking grounds. These are favourite sites within the pine forest, generally in the older woods, where each spring capercaillies come to display and to mate. The cock birds are there first, arriving well before dawn and strutting around on the ground with their tails spread and their wings trailing through the snow or on the ground, rather like turkeys. They make a weird kind of clopping noise. Someone once likened it to wine being poured out of a long-necked bottle and then the cork being pulled out with a pop! It is a very delicate noise really; you need to be close and very still to hear this peculiar sound of the woods. The Gaelic name for the capercaillie is *capull-choille*, meaning 'horse of the woods', which presumably is to do with the clopping sound made by the male in the spring – or maybe it's because of the crashing sound as the bird blunders through the forest.

In recent decades, the capercaillie has suffered a terrible decline in Scotland, with its numbers down by as much as tenfold. I remember in the early 1960s, when I first visited the pine forests around Loch Garten in Strathspey, they were a common bird. Now I am lucky if I see one or two on my walks beside that loch. They used to occur in the woods near our loch but have long since gone from there as well. The reasons are complex. They do not like wet weather and nowadays

OPPOSITE
*The capercaillie has declined in recent years
and is no longer seen in the woods near
the loch. This male is displaying in an
ancient Caledonian pine tree in another area
of the Scottish Highlands.*

we seem to have more wet and cold summers. They do not like the loss of the old pine woods either, and too many of our ancient woodlands have been felled in the last twenty years and replanted with thick conifer plantations. Sterile plantations of spruce are just not to their liking and in no way compare with the ancient forests with their rich understorey of blaeberries and heather. There are other problems as well, including too many people disturbing them at the leks, dogs walking through the woods and also an increase in predators, like crows and foxes.

At the moment, it's too early for leking and the cock capercaillies are still surviving the winter's cold. In a few weeks' time they will move away from a diet of pine needles and will go to the moss crop or bog cotton. There's a nice patch of moss crop in a little boggy area just over from the edge of the loch. In this small marsh at this time in spring the first shoots of the lovely showy cotton grass start to poke up through the dead leaves of the sedges and mosses of the mire. These spiky shoots are the first signs of spring vegetation in many parts of the Highlands. The head of the cotton grass is tightly rolled up in a blackish point, but capercaillies, roe deer and a whole range of different animals, both wild and domestic, know that this is the time to come to the mosses to pull up gently the heads of the bog cotton and savour an early bite of spring.

Merry dancers in the sky

Last night, 1 February, there was the most spectacular display of northern lights or aurora borealis. On these nights, the whole northern sky can be lit up by flashing, changing bands of green or blue or white or red lights in the sky. The northern lights this time started at about 7 p.m. It was a quiet night, quite cold, crystal clear, with sounds carrying for miles. Looking upwards, there were patterns of shadowy curtains moving across the sky, greenish, glowing and eerie. They sort of crackled, or at least you felt they crackled, as they changed direction, rather like searchlights in the night sky. As I watched, a red glow started to appear above me; in fact, as the evening progressed, it was like being inside a great dome of the deepest red or magenta, illuminated with green bands in the northern sky. These displays at times are absolutely stunning; little wonder that they are also called the 'Merry Dancers'.

Sadly, nowadays most people miss them, because they live in towns and cities, where the all-pervading orange glow of streetlights makes it impossible even to see the stars, let alone the ghostly dancers of the northern lights. These last couple of winters have been particularly good for them, but only on a few nights are they really spectacular. I am told this has to do with sun-spot activity and that the best displays occur at regular intervals of every eleven years or so. On a few occasions in the last two winters I have witnessed and enjoyed this spectacular celestial phenomenon.

Two winters ago, we had a heifer who was due to calf. In the evening she looked as though she was very close, so at 9 p.m. I went out with a torch to check progress; it was obvious that she was about to give birth to her first calf. My wife and I stood in the field and, as the newborn calf struggled to its feet for the first time, above us was the most fantastic display of the white and green shadowy curtains of the northern lights. We will always remember that special night, for we named the calf Aurora and she is still with us as part of our herd on the farm.

Birds and birchs

In all the countryside, I often feel the birch tree to be my most loyal companion. Everywhere in the woods she is with me, in her blooming, in her withering, in all her verdant glory. But most of all I love the birch because she is always there and a joy because of that. Today, her back is bent to the west wind, pale and shimmering

OVERLEAF
*Last night there was the most
spectacular display of northern lights
or aurora borealis above the loch.*

in the sleety showers with the buds beginning to swell on burgundy branches. Redpolls also love birch trees at this time of year: these little finches find plenty of food in the growing buds and later on the seeds. They're still flying around in winter flocks and in the past I have seen up to 400 together. Here, in a stand of birches just above the loch, about twenty redpolls are feeding.

Every now and then they chatter and fly around in a tiny jumping band to land in the next tree. Once landed, they almost disappear and it is very difficult to see them – they are so small, as well as being camouflaged by their streaky brown, grey and white plumage. But if you find them, feeding hanging upside down in the trees, you will see that they have the most beautiful crimson-red crowns and a really dapper little black spot, or black patch, under the bill. They also nest in the birch trees in the spring and then spread out across the countryside, a pair here and a pair there, nesting in the birches or the willows, or maybe just in a bush. Their breeding behaviour is very interesting and unique as well. Redpolls can nest in one area on the low ground early in the spring and rear young, then move several hundred miles further north and have another nest and brood later in the summer.

At the far end of the loch, where the water trickles over the dam, a heron is stalking in the shallow water. Maybe he is looking for an eel, or maybe the frogs are starting to drag themselves out of the deep insulating mud. He is looking absolutely stunning: his plumage has the most lovely silky bloom. This is a fully adult bird with the superb black drooping feathers coming away from the back of the crown. The black and white stripes down the neck are very obvious at this time of year, as are the black and white patches on the bend of the wing. The bill is very bright – really yellow, in fact. At times it is the yellowness of the bill reflecting in the water that shows exactly where the heron is walking. Sometimes he is absolutely still, frozen in mid-act, bill stretched and then, stap, he plunges into the water and a tiny little fish disappears down his throat. His mate is probably quite close by now, because herons are some of the earliest nesting birds in the Scottish Highlands.

On the way home tonight there was a slight dampness in the air, the roads shiny and wet, but it wasn't quite raining as I drove past the loch. I saw ahead of me two distinctive shapes. The first two frogs or toads of the spring were crossing the road. This is a real death trap for them, as they annually cross here from the marsh to the loch. Actually, most are toads, because they make regular short-distance migrations from their hibernating sites on land to one particular bay on the loch. When they cross the road, their little white chins catch your eye as the car headlights shine ahead. It's quite easy to miss them, although a bit like a slalom course, as you go round that one and back round another and on, and then another little jink in the road to miss one more. Sadly, some people do not realize that the frogs and toads are crossing, or maybe they don't care, for in the morning I see the squashed remains on the road.

Tired winter — new spring

It is 22 February and the pair of mute swans has already returned to the loch. They must have slipped in a day or so ago and I missed their actual return. They do not have last year's young ones with them now: they have left them down on the firth, where they will while away the summer. In fact, if the young do come back and try to land on this loch, parental responsibilities will be totally forgotten and this pair of swans will chase their previous year's young away with great determination. Sometimes they may even kill a young swan which insists on coming back the following year to the breeding loch. With them are the mallards, thirty-four in total, and if I counted them carefully I would see that there are seventeen males and seventeen females. At this time of the year, they are already paired.

In a matter of hours the weather changes again and the unpredictable nature of this climate brings a heavy snow cover to our Highland landscape. Just a few days after the toads had started to cross the road and I found my very first clump of frogspawn in a little wet hollow in the woods, it's back to winter. This is clinging snow, my dogs are covered in snowballs, especially Nell the collie dog, with her long, furry coat. The cows are dragging snowballs as big as footballs on their tails as they walk across the fields. Most animals

The grip of winter still holds onto the loch.
Frost crystals form on the birch branch.
A redpoll (above) comes down from feeding in
the birches to drink at the water's edge.

will not find this very easy snow to deal with, but hopefully it will
not last long. I was just thinking as I saw some hares running across
the field that they will not welcome this snow. Now is the time when
the hares come together and they may find it hard to be as mad as
March hares if there are 6 inches of snow on the ground. But one
knows, as the hares surely do too, that snow in March won't last
and, although their ardour may be dampened for a day, they'll soon
be back at their dancing.

Awakenings

The snows of yesterday have slipped quietly into the greening earth and there is no doubt that spring is on the way. There are snowdrops along the lochside path, there is plum blossom growing along the hedgerows as I drive towards the loch, and there is that lovely flower, the very first wild blossom in our area, called the northern butterbur. It has great big showy greenish-white flowers in the spring, but it blooms without any leaves showing. Later in the year, when the flowers have gone, large plate-sized, pale-green leaves emerge. It is the leaves that give the plant its name of butterbur, because in olden times, before fridges, deep freezes and cold stores, people in the Scottish Highlands would wrap up their butter in the leaves of this plant. The mistle thrush has started to sing; he is some distance from the loch, but somewhere on top of a high tree he is starting to tune up ready for spring.

The early evening light is fading over the loch, it is cold and windless. Suddenly there is a swoosh on the water and there amongst the mallards are three absolutely resplendent characters: a drake and two female goosanders. These ducks are larger than the mallards and are quite a different type of bird. Whereas the mallard dabbles and feeds on vegetation and seeds, frogs' eggs and scraps thrown by visitors, the goosander is a specialized fish-hunting bird. It catches its food by diving in lochs and rivers, and during winter time in the sea. The male has the most beautiful iridescent green head, with a shaggy crest on the back of the neck. The body itself is of the loveliest salmon-pink hue, with a black back, grey tail and black and white wings. The bill is long and hooked, serrated along the edge, and a bright orange-red. If you could see inside its bill, you would see that the tongue and the inside of the upper mandible are also spiked, with little spikes pointing backwards to make certain that wriggly fish do not escape once they're caught. The female is a duller bird, but still very beautiful. She is pale grey all over, slightly paler underneath, with a white flash in the wing and a pale whitish front. Most distinctively, she has a beautiful chestnut-brown head, with a rather similar crest to the males as well as a white chin. She has the same striking bill as her mate.

WINTER

These birds do not nest on our loch and I am not sure why they are here, because this is not a favourite site for goosanders. Maybe they were *en route* from the coast to the inland rivers and lochs and decided to stop off here to roost for just one night. Nevertheless, there is no time to waste and the male bird starts a stunning display. He rushes at the two females and there is just terrific excitement with birds stretching their heads upwards and then rapidly downwards, standing in the water, plunging at each other, diving shallowly under water, splashing and often calling with the most unusual long, low, bell-like wooden creaking call. It is the most beautiful courtship display and undoubtedly they have no interest in me.

When the goosander female is ready to lay her eggs, she will search out a hollow tree, somewhere along the river far up in the glens, and there she will lay her eggs. She is a tree-nesting bird, rather than a ground nester like the closely related red-breasted merganser, and when the eggs are hatched, after nearly a month of incubation, the ducklings will have to jump out of the nest hole and land on the ground below. Once the eggs are laid, the male birds have nothing more to do with home life and leave to join up on lochs in the area.

For goosanders, June is the time to think of moulting and then the most curious thing happens. All the drakes which nest in the Scottish Highlands join up with those from the rest of Britain and head off across the North Sea, across the southern tip of Scandinavia, up through the Baltic Sea and on to the Arctic Ocean. Their destination is Varanger Fjord in the very north of Norway. This is a place of plentiful food and the drake goosanders spend their summer here, slowly moulting into their eclipse plumage, then moulting their flight feathers and for a while becoming totally flightless on the sea. Slowly, as summer turns into autumn, they regain their full splendid plumage and make the return flight of several thousand miles back to Scotland.

OVERLEAF
Birch trees silhouetted by a
dramatic winter sunrise.

Generally, our local goosanders make for the Beauly Firth near Inverness, where they meet their females and the young birds that have been reared that year. The first goosander nested in Scotland in 1871 and, since then, they have spread throughout the rest of the country. Those first birds must have been immigrants from Scandinavia and the species has maintained the ancestral moult migration all the way to northern Norway ever since. It is one of the most astounding migrations that I know.

Journey's end

It is just the very start of March, not yet officially spring, because spring is supposed not to come until 21 March, but I always think that once certain spring migrants come back, like lapwings, oystercatchers, curlews and black-headed gulls, then spring is here whatever the date. Despite the fact there will still be cold, wintry days, the season has actually changed and this was underlined today when I was feeding the cattle. Suddenly there was a little 'chisick, chisick' and back came my pied wagtail. I call it my pied wagtail: it isn't really my pied wagtail, but it is undoubtedly the pied wagtail that nests amongst the farm buildings. Last year, the pair nested under a sheet of tin which was lying on the ground, and they reared five young. This bird today is absolutely spick and span, like a dapper little gentleman dressed in black and white, as he struts amongst the feet of the cattle, picking up insects where the cows have churned up the ground. Once the pied wagtail is back, then in my view spring has started and winter is at an end.

THE NEW HARTFORD MEMORIAL LIBRARY
P.O. Box 247
Central Avenue at Town Hill Road
New Hartford, Connecticut 06057
(860) 379-7235